T0311756

Cambridge Elements ☰

Elements in the Politics of Development
edited by
Rachel Beatty Riedl
Einaudi Center for International Studies and Cornell University
Ben Ross Schneider
Massachusetts Institute of Technology

Mario Einaudi
CENTER FOR
INTERNATIONAL STUDIES

 MIT CENTER FOR INTERNATIONAL STUDIES

VARIETIES
OF NATIONALISM

Communities, Narratives, Identities

Harris Mylonas
The George Washington University

Maya Tudor
University of Oxford

 CAMBRIDGE
UNIVERSITY PRESS

Shaftesbury Road, Cambridge CB2 8EA, United Kingdom

One Liberty Plaza, 20th Floor, New York, NY 10006, USA

477 Williamstown Road, Port Melbourne, VIC 3207, Australia

314–321, 3rd Floor, Plot 3, Splendor Forum, Jasola District Centre, New Delhi – 110025, India

103 Penang Road, #05–06/07, Visioncrest Commercial, Singapore 238467

Cambridge University Press is part of Cambridge University Press & Assessment, a department of the University of Cambridge.

We share the University's mission to contribute to society through the pursuit of education, learning and research at the highest international levels of excellence.

www.cambridge.org
Information on this title: www.cambridge.org/9781108972925

DOI: 10.1017/9781108973298

© Harris Mylonas and Maya Tudor 2023

This publication is in copyright. Subject to statutory exception and to the provisions of relevant collective licensing agreements, no reproduction of any part may take place without the written permission of Cambridge University Press & Assessment.

First published 2023

A catalogue record for this publication is available from the British Library.

ISBN 978-1-108-97292-5 Paperback
ISSN 2515-1584 (online)
ISSN 2515-1576 (print)

Cambridge University Press & Assessment has no responsibility for the persistence or accuracy of URLs for external or third-party internet websites referred to in this publication and does not guarantee that any content on such websites is, or will remain, accurate or appropriate.

Varieties of Nationalism

Communities, Narratives, Identities

Elements in the Politics of Development

DOI: 10.1017/9781108973298
First published online: June 2023

Harris Mylonas
The George Washington University

Maya Tudor
University of Oxford

Author for correspondence: Harris Mylonas, harris.mylonas@gmail.com

Abstract: Nationalism has long been a normatively and empirically contested concept, associated with democratic revolutions and public goods provision, but also with xenophobia, genocide, and wars. Moving beyond facile distinctions between "good" and "bad" nationalisms, the authors argue that nationalism is an empirically variegated ideology. Definitional disagreements, Eurocentric conceptualizations, and linear associations between ethnicity and nationalism have hampered our ability to synthesize insights. This Element proposes that nationalism can be broken down productively into parts based on three key questions: (1) Does a nation exist? (2) How do national narratives vary? (3) When do national narratives matter? The answers to these questions generate five dimensions along which nationalism varies: elite fragmentation and popular fragmentation of national communities; ascriptiveness and thickness of national narratives; and salience of national identities.

This Element also has a video abstract: Cambridge.org/Mylonas/Tudor_abstract

Keywords: nationalism, nations, narratives, identity, communities

© Harris Mylonas and Maya Tudor 2023

ISBNs: 9781108972925 (PB), 9781108973298 (OC)
ISSNs: 2515-1584 (online), 2515-1576 (print)

Contents

1 Why Another Nationalism Book?   1

2 What We Already Know about Nationalism   15

3 Does a Nation Exist?   30

4 How Do National Narratives Vary?   42

5 When Do National Narratives Matter?   49

6 Nationalism across Social Science Disciplines   51

7 Conclusion   59

References   64

1 Why Another Nationalism Book?

A group of blind men heard that a strange animal, called an elephant, had been brought to the town, but none of them were aware of its shape and form. Out of curiosity, they said: "We must inspect and know it by touch, of which we are capable." So, they sought it out, and when they found it, they groped about it. The first person, whose hand landed on the trunk, said, "This being is like a thick snake." For another one whose hand reached its ear, it seemed like a kind of fan. As for another person, whose hand was upon its leg, said, the elephant is a pillar like a tree-trunk. The blind man who placed his hand upon its side said the elephant, "is a wall." Another who felt its tail, described it as a rope. The last felt its tusk, stating the elephant is that which is hard, smooth and like a spear.

Tittha Sutha, ancient Buddhist text (500 BCE)

It may, indeed, be one of the tragic dimensions of human life that we can neither do without the political promulgation and institutionalization of "stories of people-hood" nor can we hope to eradicate entirely their virulent potential.

Rogers Smith (2003)

This Element is a guide for how to think about each country's unique experience with nationalism while also allowing for more general comparisons across varieties of nationalism. Nationalism is the most powerful political ideology of the modern age. Arising first in early modern Western Europe,[1] nationalism diffused slowly throughout the rest of Europe in the eighteenth and nineteenth centuries and was nearly universally adopted by the twentieth century. Nationalism has been intrinsic-ally linked with the horrors of World War II, but also the decolonization movements following World War II. Today, no other political doctrine commands such global popularity as that a people should be self-determined and sovereign. Nationalism has come to define modernity both by shaping the international system of nation-states and by regulating individual loyalty and solidarity within the confines of a nation.

Beyond structuring our inter*national* system and constituting national communities over the past two centuries,[2] nationalism has recently reshaped domestic politics in every corner of the globe. India's Narendra Modi swept to power in 2014 and 2019 through election campaigns explicitly touting Hindu nationalism, creating what is broadly understood to be a new dominant party system.[3] In 2016, Britain's then-prime minister, Theresa May, underscored the importance of national citizenship by arguing "If you believe you are a citizen of the world, you are a citizen of nowhere. You don't understand what 'citizenship' means."[4]

---

[1] Gorski 2000.   [2] Mylonas and Kuo 2018; Jenne and Mylonas 2023.

[3] Chhibber and Verma 2018; Ziegfeld 2020; Dayal 2021.

[4] Bearak 2016. Other recent, relevant examples of the importance of nationalism include the independence referendums in Scotland and Catalonia as well as the ascendant anti-EU nationalist sentiment in Hungary and Poland.

That same year, Donald Trump was elected president of the United States after promising in his campaign to "Make America Great Again" and put "America First."[5] In 2018, Brazil's Jair Bolsonaro invoked Trump's discourse, running a campaign to "make Brazil great again" that saw him win the presidency. And China's Xi Jinping has pushed for a Han-centric understanding of Chinese nationalism to consolidate his power to such a degree that he is widely considered the most powerful leader of the People's Republic of China since Mao Zedong.[6]

If Donald Trump's "Make America Great Again" motto exemplified the global trend of reawakening nationalism as a campaigning force, the defeats of Trump and Bolsonaro do not obviate the nationalist trend. It suffices to remember that to defeat Trump, President Biden's efforts centered around reclaiming the definition of patriotism in the USA referring to "Build(ing) Back Better" and the "Battle for the Soul of the Nation."[7] While these nationalisms differ in important respects, there is little doubt that politicians overtly embracing nationalist rhetoric were an unanticipated political trend across the globe, a trend which flew in the face of Western liberals who expected and predicted that nationalism would die a natural death with "the end of history." [8]

The contemporary reawakening of nationalism in domestic politics is also linked to the rise of *economic* nationalism – policies seeking to delimit trade flows, champion national industry, and disengage from international economic cooperation. Following the disintegration of the Soviet Union, in which nationalism played a key role,[9] global leaders largely accepted that "history"–or ideological competition between capitalist democracies and economically centralized autocracies – had ended and been replaced with the ideological consensus that capitalism, globalism, and liberal democracy had triumphed.[10] Economically, this meant that international organizations such as the World Bank and the International Monetary Fund pursued "Washington Consensus" policies – for example, market-determined exchange rates, trade liberalization, and fiscal discipline – that promoted globalization by opening up overseas markets to unfettered capital flows. Consequently, Latin America, Eastern Europe, South Asia, and sub-Saharan Africa witnessed more trade liberalization during the 1990s and early 2000s than any other point in modern history.[11] This changed during the 2010s, as the Washington Consensus was challenged by economic nationalism exemplified by Trump's trade war with China and by Britain's exodus from the European Union. Today, advanced and emerging

---

[5] Bhambra 2017; Goldstein and Hall 2017. For the trope see Levinger and Lytle 2001.
[6] Blackwill and Campbell 2016, Brown 2017.   [7] Biden 2022.   [8] Fukuyama 1989.
[9] Suny 1993; Beissinger 2002.   [10] Boix 2019.
[11] See Williamson (2000) and Rodrik (2006). East Asian tigers notably liberalized earlier; see the World Bank Policy Research Report, *The East Asia Miracle* (1993).

economies alike are moving toward policies of economic nationalism, albeit at different speeds.[12]

The 2020 outbreak of the global coronavirus pandemic only accentuated the nation-state's place as the primary site of policymaking.[13] A pandemic that paradoxically underscored the interconnected nature of our governments, economies, and environments caused government leaders to invoke national solidarity while announcing nation-specific measures to limit the spread of the pandemic, including border closures. The crisis' most consequential actor was the national state, with its broad array of economic, welfare and organizational powers. Even in the supranational European Union, the nearest embodiment of the nation-state's transcendence, border closures happened largely in an uncoordinated, state-led fashion. As the distribution of vaccines was the responsibility of nation-states and national health-care systems,[14] the coronavirus pandemic has forced a reassertion of the nation-state. As right-wing British nationalist Nigel Farage quipped early on in the pandemic, "we are all nationalists now."[15]

The Russian invasion of Ukraine has also highlighted the enduring relevance (and empirical duality) of nationalism 'at the international level.' A critical cause for the invasion of Ukraine, as articulated by Vladimir Putin, was his understanding of Russian national identity that dictated the denial of a Ukrainian national identity:[16] "Russians and Ukrainians were one people – a single whole . . . modern Ukraine is entirely the product of the Soviet era. We know and remember well that it was shaped – for a significant part – on the lands of historical Russia."[17] Putin cited Ukrainian state policies against the use of the Russian language in Ukraine, attempts of instilling anti-Russian sentiments, and the breakdown of relations between the Ukrainian and Russian Orthodox Churches in justifying his invasion, suggesting that Ukrainian President Zelensky's goal was "forced assimilation, the formation of an ethnically pure Ukrainian state, aggressive towards Russia, was comparable in its consequences to the use of weapons of mass destruction against us." His concluding statement underscored how relevant nationalism was to the war's motivation: "Our kinship has been transmitted from generation to generation. It is in the hearts and the memory of people living in modern Russia and Ukraine, in the blood ties that unite millions of our families. Together we have always been and will be many times stronger and more successful. For we are one people." Putin's ascriptive understanding of Russianness is at the heart of his political actions.[18]

---

[12] De Bolle and Zettelmeyer 2019.   [13] Bieber 2022; Mylonas and Whalley 2022.
[14] Kamradt-Scott 2020.   [15] Farage 2020.   [16] Kuzio 2016; Hill 2022.   [17] Putin 2021.
[18] Hill and Stent 2022.

But if Putin's concept of Russian nationhood motivated the war, Ukrainian nationalism has united the Ukrainian people in a more inclusive understanding of nationhood and spurred on the defense of the country's newfound democracy.[19] And it is for this reason that Ukrainian nationalism has been widely embraced throughout Europe and the United States, with cultural symbols such as the Eiffel Tower, Brandenburg Gate, London Eye, and the Empire State Building being lit up with the Ukrainian flag.

1.1 Addressing Five Problems in Nationalism Scholarship

Despite the growing importance of nationalism both domestically and internationally and a clear need for empirically driven assessments, scholars of nationalism are surprisingly inconsistent in their definitional and conceptual approaches. *The first problem we therefore hope to address is the paucity of definitional discussions of nationalism.* It is common practice among scholars of democracy to specify their own definition of democracy in relation to other scholarship at the outset of their research process.[20] In contrast to the democracy scholarship, nationalism scholars employ a broad range of definitions without engaging with or relating to one another's definitions. As Hutchinson and Smith aptly put it "perhaps the central difficulty in the study of nations and nationalism has been the problem of finding adequate and agreed definitions of the key concepts of nation and nationalism." (1994: 4).

Even among nationalism's most-cited scholars, its definition varies widely, including an imagined community, an ideological movement, a state of mind, and collective action. While such definitions *can* be related to one another and while we do not need a single universal definition of nationalism, the lack of attention to definitions has led to widespread confusion. Indeed, Connor (1994: 91) writes that the term nationalism "is shrouded in ambiguity due to [scholars'] imprecise, inconsistent and often totally erroneous usage," while Tishkov (2000: 625–650) goes so far as to suggest eschewing the terms "nation" and "nationalism" altogether because they are conceptually meaningless. To remedy this widespread confusion, nationalism scholars need henceforth to situate their understanding of nationalism vis-à-vis established definitions and strive for definitional clarity at the outset of their research.

The conceptual and definitional confusion arises partly because nationalism scholarship spans the disciplines of history, anthropology, political science, psychology, and sociology and partly because nationalism scholarship often

---

[19] Kulyk 2014; Zhuravlev and Ishchenko 2020; Onuch and Hale 2022.
[20] See for example, Coppedge 2002; Munck and Verkuilen 2002.

relies on single case studies. Consequently, "subtypes" of nationalism have proliferated. This definitional disagreement is exacerbated by the fact some scholars study nationalism at the political unit level, others at the community level, while yet others at the individual level. Unsurprisingly then, much like the blind men who each describe the elephant based on the part they hold, such an approach has led to a dizzying proliferation of understandings of nationalism. Since nationalism scholars rarely devote substantial time to definitional clarity, cumulative scholarly knowledge remains necessarily sparse.

For example, a Google Scholar search for "nationalism" yields the following qualifiers of nationalism in the top 100 book/journal titles alone: affective, consumer, cosmopolitan, digital, imperial, irredentist, nostalgic, nativist, popular, resource, restorative, religious, tribal, and vaccine.[21] "Nationalism with adjectives" has become the norm.[22] Sometimes, the use of such qualifiers can helpfully move us down the ladder of conceptual abstraction – when the qualifying adjectives are used to emphasize contextually specific empirical patterns of nationalism. Yet, especially when these qualifiers are not clearly defined and justified in relation to other scholars' work, adding qualifiers can stretch the concept of nationalism so far that it loses analytical meaning.[23] More generally, nationalism scholarship that neither specifies its conceptual foundations nor delineates which dimension of nationalism is being observed or measured generates a medley of empirical findings that rarely advances our knowledge.[24] It is precisely because nationalism can vary across contexts and over time that we need a well-specified discussion of the dimensions along which national communities, national narratives, and national identities vary.[25]

Addressing such imprecision is also made difficult because, as we discuss in greater depth in Section 2, nationalism has three core attributes: (1) an intersubjective recognition and celebration of an imagined community as a locus of loyalty and solidarity, (2) a drive for sovereign self-rule over a distinct territory pursued by a significant segment of a group's elite, and (3) a repertoire of symbols and practices that embody the nation. These attributes are bundled

---

[21] Chang 1998; Ding and Hlavac 2017.

[22] During the 1990s, democracy was a similarly defined with respect to a hodgepodge of adjectives until Collier and Levitsky (1997) wrote their seminal article calling for conceptual clarity on the term. We pursue a similar aim with respect to nationalism.

[23] Sartori 1970.

[24] Abdelal et al. (2009) are an exception. In *Measuring Identity*, they emphasize two main dimensions of identity: content and contestation. The contestation dimension is similar to our fragmentation dimension. Their "content" dimension is analogous to our "ascriptiveness" dimension, except that they identify four types of content: constitutive norms, social purposes, relational comparisons, and cognitive models

[25] Barrington 1997.

together since the intersubjective recognition and celebration of an imagined community is partly constituted by a shared repertoire of symbols, while the pursuit of sovereignty is often built on an awareness of belonging to this imagined community. Yet the precise characteristics defining membership in one national community in one case may be irrelevant in another case. Though a shared language, religion, ethnicity, and natural geographical borders can all be associated with particular understandings of nationhood, national narratives that lack each of these characteristics abound. As nations and nationalisms have a Wittgenstein-like "family resemblance" in which no one characteristic is essential,[26] aiming for Sartori-like precision in our conceptual understanding of nationalism may be futile. Definitions of nations and nationalism will necessarily remain broad.[27] But some conceptual clarity is possible and should be attempted – and that is our aim in *Varieties of Nationalism*.

A second problem we seek to address is the conceptual confusion created by the putative link between nationalism and ethnicity. We argue that scholars of nationalism should henceforth firmly delink definitions of nationalism from ethnicity.[28] As Table 1 also shows, scholars are inconsistent about whether they definitionally link nationalism to ethnicity. Particularly because the concept of "ethnicity" can in some cases be taken to encompass race and caste, scholarly usage of the term has stretched well beyond common usage of the term.[29] Moreover, while nationalism *may* use ethnicity as its building block, there are clearly nations and nationalisms which do not build upon an ethnicity. Stipulating instead that nationalism is defined by an intersubjective recognition of a nation; the drive for sovereign self-rule over a distinct territory; and a repertoire of symbols brings the public usage of "nationalism" into alignment with contemporary scholarship, which shows that at least some nations have been created without emphasizing their links to a particular ethnic group. While some scholars will contend that nationalisms require ethnicity, such scholars should also specify their understanding of ethnicity, since the term is also subject to a wide range of contested meanings.[30]

A third problem we seek to address is the Eurocentric bias of mainstream nationalism scholarship. Classical scholars of nationalism, including Hans Kohn, John Breuilly, Ernest Gellner, Liah Greenfeld, and Anthony Smith,

---

[26] Wittgenstein 2001(1953). The philosopher Ludwig Wittgenstein argued that entities that may be thought to be connected by one essential feature may be in fact connected by a series of overlapping similarities with no one feature being common to all of those entities.

[27] Sartori 1970. Giovanni Sartori was an Italian political scientist that highlighted the problem of concept misformation.

[28] For an excellent article on the lack of consensus on what ethnicity is, see Hale 2004.

[29] Green 2006.   [30] Green 2006.

Table 1 Commonly cited definitions of nationalism

Scholar	Definition of nationalism	Relationship to ethnicity?
Benedict Anderson (1983: 36, 6)	"[a] new way of linking fraternity, power and time meaningfully together" by constructing "an imagined political community – and imagined as both inherently limited and sovereign."	Not definitionally necessary.
Walker Connor (1994: xi)	"Nation connotes a group of people who believe they are ancestrally related. Nationalism connotes identification with and loyalty to one's nation as just defined."	Essential.
Ernest Gellner (1983: 1)	"[p]rimarily a political principle, which holds that the political and the national unit should be congruent."	Not definitionally necessary.
Liah Greenfeld (1992: Back cover)	"Nationalism is a movement and a state of mind that brings together national identity, consciousness, and collectivities."	Not definitionally necessary, but empirically often linked.
Michael Hechter (2000: 7, 14)	"Collective action designed to render the boundaries of the nation congruent with those of its governance unit."[. . .] "Nations[. . .] constitute a subset of ethnic groups. They are territorially concentrated ethnic groups"	Essential.
Anthony Smith (1999: 18)	"Nationalism is a modern ideological movement, but also the expression of aspirations by various social groups to create, defend or maintain nations — their autonomy, unity and identity — by drawing on the cultural resources of pre-existing ethnic communities and categories."	Essential.

mostly theorized in their canonical monographs of nationalism from cases in Europe and the Americas.[31] Yet, early European and American national-isms do not represent the majority of today's nationalisms. European nation-states may have been the first to emerge and were certainly worthy of intensive study. But European nation-states are now outliers in the sense that most non-European states legitimating their authority through nationalism did not emerge after a protracted process of state-building, as was true of the canonical European cases of England and France. Many nation-states in the Americas were founded by what Anderson calls "creole pioneers" – colonists that staged rebellions against the imperial metropole mainly in reaction to their blocked social mobility at the imperial center.[32] While most nation-states of the world emerged through a distinctly twentieth-century process whereby Indigenous elites borrowed a language of nationalism to legitimize their power and ambitions to control former colonial states; when such elites embraced narratives of "we the people," they sometimes built national communities without introducing mass literacy, without having capacious states, and without relying on ethnic building blocks. Lisa Wedeen (2008), for instance, describes such a case in her book on Yemen. In this Element, by theoriz-ing from a broad range of work that has examined the emergence of both European and postcolonial nationalisms, we provide a more robust orien-tation that we are confident applies to nationalisms across the globe.

A fourth problem we address, related to Eurocentricism, are the strong normative biases in the literature on nationalism. One such bias comes from scholars' own contextually-specific experiences with nationalism. For instance, whereas thinkers from continental Europe, and especially Germany, tend to abjectly reject nationalism as a positive force, English thinkers tend to have more positive views of nationalism.[33] The majority of published scholarly works on nationalism are either normative treatises or empirical investigations of a single country's nationalism or nationalist episodes. Yet the broad range of empirical findings already suggest that nationalism is a Janus-faced phenom-enon. And any argument suggesting that nationalism is likely to have *general* types of effects must invariably be built on comparative foundations, either across a broad geographical set of cases or over time. A consensus exists that

---

[31] Benedict Anderson is an exception as much of his work was on South East Asia.

[32] Anderson 1983, chapter 4.

[33] See for example, Jürgen Habermas 1976 as the preeminent German voice on nationalism and David Miller 1995 as the preeminent English voice on nationalism.

"cross-national research is valuable, even indispensible for establishing the generality of findings and the validity of interpretations."[34]

Fifth, and finally, we hope to help balance the scholarly focus on the historical origins of nationalism by drawing our attention to systematic comparisons of nationalism's consequences at different levels: community, narrative, individual. Scholars have engaged in dialogue about the *comparative* consequences of nationalism. But a majority of classic works on nationalism are case studies and of those, mostly investigations into nationalism's origins. Particularly because there is such public and scholarly debate about nationalism's origins, much more work is needed to better understand nationalism's consequences. By providing a set of questions and dimensions along which nationalisms vary, we provide a framework for scholars hoping to undertake careful empirical comparative research into nationalism's consequences.

1.2 Our Framework: One Definition, Three Questions, and Five Dimensions

In *Varieties of Nationalism*, we provide a guide for how to think about nations and nationalism in general terms, allowing both for recognition of each country's particularities and broad comparisons across countries. Despite the fact that the term "nation" is etymologically derived from the Latin word *natio* – denoting birth or origin – we hold that nationalism is *not* necessarily linked to attributes associated with, or believed to be associated with descent or ethnicity.[35] We understand nationalism as an intersubjective awareness of an imagined community together with a meaningful degree of collective action to attain self-rule and full sovereignty over a particular territory for this community.[36]

To be clear, for a sentiment/identity to qualify as nationalism/nationalist, it *must* include an aspiration for sovereignty over a particular territory at least by a significant segment of elites or members of a community.[37] For example, Bavarian *nationalism* in Germany does not practically exist because there is no

---

[34] Kohn 1987.   [35] Chandra 2006.

[36] In this book we focus primarily on two types of sovereignty: Westphalian sovereignty – referring to political organization based on the exclusion of external actors from authority structures within a given territory – and domestic sovereignty, which refers to the formal organization of political authority within the state and the ability of rulers to exercise control within it. For more on the concept of sovereignty, see Krasner 1999.

[37] Following Wimmer and Feinstein (2010), we identify nationalist movements as political organizations in which the membership is formally defined, the leadership roles are institutionalized, the representation of the relevant national community as a whole is claimed, and the goal is to achieve either independence or autonomy.

significant segment of the population or elites that advocates for secession from the sovereign state of Germany. This does not mean that there is not awareness of a Bavarian identity, but because this identity is not associated with a drive for full sovereignty, it does not meet the criteria to be called "nationalist." Quebec or Québécois nationalism, by contrast, existed to such a degree throughout the 1980s and 1990s that two referenda for political independence from Canada were held, the latter of which came within a percentage point of attaining sovereignty. Kashmiri nationalism exists, with a substantial portion of elites seeking independence from India (and Pakistan). Comparisons between Scottish and Welsh nationalism are also relevant here, since substantial movements advocating political independence from the United Kingdom – a sovereign state – exist in the form of the Scottish National Party (SNP) and Plaid Cymru, respectively, though surveys establish that Plaid Cymru has less popular support than the SNP. Most states, especially federal ones, will have multiple political identities available for mobilization. But this does not mean that all political identities are national.[38] To do so, substantial organized interests must take the form of national movements seeking political sovereignty. We elaborate on this definition in the next section.

The core argument we develop below is that more conceptual clarity around nationalism is needed and that this can be gained by breaking down nationalism into constituent parts based on three general questions: (1) Does a nation exist? (2) How do national narratives vary? (3) When do national narratives matter to individuals? These questions, which correspond to Sections 3, 4, and 5 respectively, meaningfully capture much of the comparative variation in nationalisms identified by different scholars. Confusion often ensues when scholars talk past each other *exactly because* they are addressing different questions within nationalism scholarship. National communities can have varied degrees of cohesion,[39] their national narratives come in great range of building blocks,[40] and these national identities can be more or less salient for different individuals or groups at any given point in time.[41] As Figure 1 indicates, situating nationalism scholarship with respect to these three questions can help scholars to overcome the muddled conceptual problems we identified above and describe the particularities of nationalisms across space and over time.

---

[38] Federalisms can varyingly accommodate national identities, see Amoretti and Bermeo 2004.

[39] Reeskens and Wright 2012.   [40] Smith 2003; Aktürk 2012; Brand 2014.

[41] Charnysh et al. 2015; Wimmer 2018.

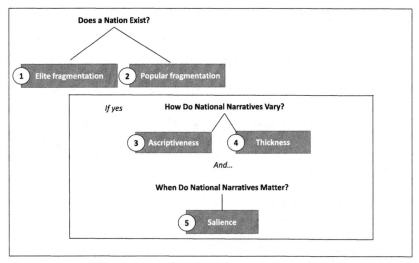

Figure 1 The five dimensions of nationalism

In *Varieties of Nationalism*, we argue that nationalism is a phenomenon which existing scholarship has already shown to vary, in response to our three questions, along five dimensions: *elite and popular fragmentation of national communities; ascriptiveness and thickness of national narratives; and salience of national identities*. Specifically, national communities can be characterized by *popular* and/or *elite fragmentation* – capturing the degree to which elites and popular definitions of the nation are commonly held or are alternatively fragmented. In turn, national communities are characterized by important variation in national narratives. Different understandings of nationhood or national narratives can vary by their *ascriptiveness* – or the degree to which national belonging is determined by purportedly inheritable categories such as race, ethnicity, or in some cases religion. The *thickness* of markers that define membership to a nation – ranging from relatively thin in the case of shared geographical borders to thicker overlapping cultural markers of ethnicity, language, and religion – is yet another way that national narratives may vary.[42] And finally, the *salience* of national identities relative to other sub- or supranational identities also varies (tending to rise around events such as wars, important national sports victories, and the death of a monarch).

---

[42] Note that the way we use the term "thickness" parts ways from Geertz's (1973) or Hale's (2004) understanding of "thick," that is, high levels of meaning. Geertz's conceptualization is closer to what we term "salience" of national identities. We use the term "thickness" to signify the richness of symbolism and the number of layers that a national narrative involves.

Consider this writer chronicling the transformation of her national identity during the breakdown of Yugoslavia:[43]

> Being Croat has become my destiny... I am defined by my nationality, and by it alone... Along with millions of other Croats, I was pinned to the wall of nationhood – not only by outside pressure from Serbia and the Federal Army but by national homogenization within Croatia itself. That is what the war is doing to us, reducing us to one dimension: the Nation. The trouble with this nationhood, however, is that whereas before, I was defined by my education, my job, my ideas, my character – and, yes, my nationality too – now I feel stripped of all that. I am nobody because I am not a person anymore. I am one of 4.5 million Croats... I am not in a position to choose any longer. Nor, I think, is anyone else... something people cherished as a part of their cultural identity – an alternative to the all-embracing communism... – has become their political identity and turned into something like an ill-fitting shirt. You may feel the sleeves are too short, the collar too tight. You might not like the colour, and the cloth might itch. But there is no escape; there is nothing else to wear. One doesn't have to succumb voluntarily to this ideology of the nation – one is sucked into it. So right now, in the new state of Croatia, no one is allowed not to be a Croat.[44]

How are we to conceptualize and measure this seismic change from Yugoslavian to Croatian nationalism? Before assessing any change, the *first* question is whether a Yugoslav (literally meaning south Slav) national community existed? Such an identity did exist, because research instantiated that elites and popular voices understood, identified with, and (to varying degrees) promoted a Yugoslav national identity. Moreover, some Yugoslavs did identify with Yugoslavia as their primary national identity by the 1980s.[45] Thus, there was some *popular* and *elite consensus* around the existence of a Yugoslav national identity.

The *second* question is what is the content of Yugoslavia's founding narrative of peoplehood? Yugoslavia as a country came into existence in the twentieth century following World War I and the collapse of Austria-Hungary and the Ottoman Empire. It was initially called the Kingdom of Serbs, Croats, and Slovenes, but King Aleksandar changed the name into Kingdom of Yugoslavia at the start of 1929. Its founding moment came about because of Slovenian and Croatian fears of Italian domination, coupled with the long-lasting desire of Serbian intellectuals and high ranking officers to unite all the Serbs into a single state, which led to the unification of the South Slavs.[46] The interwar years involved a series of efforts by Serbia's political leaders to turn the new kingdom into a centralized state under Serbian hegemony. Following World War

[43] Banac 1984.   [44] Drakulic 1993: 50–52.   [45] Kukic 2019.
[46] Mylonas 2012: 154; Malešević 2019: Chapter 8.

II, Josip Broz Tito was the chief architect of the Socialist Federal Republic of Yugoslavia (SFRY). The post– World War II Yugoslav national narrative was a capacious identity that encompassed a range of national and ethnic identities.[47] Yugoslavia was a multinational federation comprised of several nationalities with equal rights, but Tito was also nurturing a supranational Yugoslav identity.[48] In sum then, at the time that Slavenka Drakulić was writing the quote above, Yugoslav nationalism was *thinly defined and layered over multiple nationalities and generally it was not ascriptively defined.*

Finally, the *third* question relates to the salience of the Yugoslav national identity. Surveys show that the salience of Yugoslav national identity appeared to be relatively low before the breakout of the civil wars during Yugoslavia's disintegration,[49] after which time the salience of ethnocultural definitions of the nation rose.[50] *The salience of the Yugoslav national identity was relatively low and remained low, while the salience of ethnoculturally defined national identities in the country (i.e., Serbs, Croats, Slovenes, etc.) rose during and after the 1990s Yugoslav wars.*[51]

Through the process of conflict, Yugoslavian nationalism saw greater *elite* and *popular fragmentation*, though sorting out cause and consequence remains tricky.[52] A less *ascriptive* Yugoslav national narrative was replaced by more ascriptive national identities, as *ethnic* belonging became the most prominent determinant of group membership in former Yugoslavia. And undoubtedly the writer above suggested the growing *salience* of her national Croatian identity. In short, this moment in history reflected a change in *all* facets of Yugoslav nationalism – changes that most theoretical discussions of nationalism do not clearly disentangle.

Yet other moments of history may involve a change in just one dimension of nationalism. The advent of World War II in Europe, for example, witnessed the rising salience of the French national identity relative to other identities in the country through a well-known "rally around the flag" effect, even as the degree of elite and popular fragmentation of the French national community or the ascriptiveness or thickness of the French national narrative remained unchanged. In the last decade, under the leadership of Narendra Modi, India's national narrative has become both more ascriptive (practically equated with Hinduism) and more salient (since the government repeatedly invokes this definition of the nation).[53] Nationalism scholars should clearly identify which part of nationalism they are studying as well as which dimension(s) they are focusing on.

---

[47] Ramet 1992; Wachtel 1998; Sekulić 2004.
[48] For more on how ethno-national identities were seen as the building blocks of the Yugoslav political project, see Malešević 2002.
[49] Sekulić et al. 1994.   [50] Dyrstad 2012; Kukic 2019.   [51] Baker 2015.   [52] Somer 2001.
[53] Tudor 2018, 2023.

These five dimensions of nationalism meaningfully capture the major ways in which scholars have approached nationalism to date. While we cannot preclude the possibility that future research will uncover additional consequential dimensions of variance, existing scholarship both instantiates that nationalisms vary along these five dimensions and employs such variance to explain important phenomena in political science such as state capacity, political violence, immigration and asylum policies, regime outcomes, and public goods provision.

Much like scholars of regime types are asked to delineate their definitions and types of democracy so that scholarship can be conceptually cumulative,[54] scholars of nationalism should lay out their conceptual definitions and empirical measurements of nationalism. Considering the different dimensions along which national communities and their national narratives vary is a first step in an integrated empirical examination of the elephant that is nationalism.

1.3 A Road Map

The broad aim of this Element is to encourage scholars studying nationalism to carefully relate their research questions to these major dimensions of nationalism. To be sure, there are many dimensions of nationalism that may matter for outcomes which we do not discuss, just as elephants may have many physical dimensions. Yet we have included here the dimensions of nationalism that scholars have found to consistently vary over time and across regions in ways that have critical consequences. For if researchers are to arrive at a rigorous empirical evaluation of nationalism's variegated origins and effects, the dimensions along which national communities, narratives, and identities vary must be defined and operationalized in a clear, consistent manner. Much like the different parts of the blind man's elephant, nationalism can assume immensely different shapes.

The remainder of the Element is structured as follows: Section 2 distills what we know about nationalism's origins, presents key definitions, and delineates its relationship with other major ideologies. In Section 3, we argue that when national imagined communities emerge, their survival critically hinges upon two dimensions: elite and popular fragmentation. We also discuss how variation along these dimensions affects a range of important societal outcomes ranging from state capacity and political violence to democracy and public goods provision. In Section 4, we turn our focus on how national narratives vary along the two dimensions of ascriptiveness and thickness, and how these dimensions of variance map onto consequential political outcomes.

---

[54] Collier and Levitsky 1997.

In Section 5, we turn our attention at the individual level and how national identities can vary in their salience. Section 6 draws upon the insights of disciplines as diverse as history, political science, sociology, philosophy, psychology, and evolutionary biology to supplement our understanding of nationalism. Section 7 concludes with a call for a more explicitly comparative and cumulative research agenda.

2 What We Already Know about Nationalism

A century ago, the world was comprised of fewer than sixty countries and a motley assortment of kingdoms, city-states, and empires. Today, nearly 200 countries have almost entirely replaced these older political units. The nationalist revolution represents the largest political transformation in modern history. A wide range of political forms morphed into the preeminent political actor of our age – a state representing or claiming to represent a nation.[55] Even amidst the powerful new forces of globalization and digital connectivity, the state – more often than not legitimated through the ideology of nationalism – remains our most consequential actor for addressing the world's pressing policy challenges, from inequality and poverty to climate change, war, and global pandemics.

Despite the continued relevance of nationalism as a key organizing political principle, the study of nationalism is still comparatively sparse and dispersed in political science. Figure 2 measures the frequency of words in English-language books since 1800 and shows that the mention of the term "democracy" is at least twice as popular as "nationalism," and the term "political parties" almost four times as prevalent as "nationalism."

Yet there is little doubt that nationalism is as important as these other concepts, for the states which lie at the heart of our world system are ultimately

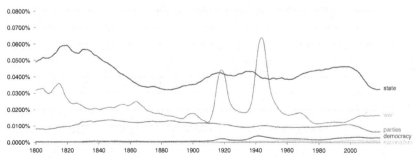

Figure 2 Frequency of "nationalism" and other terms in books, 1800 to 2019

---

[55] Spruyt (1994).

legitimated by a sense of solidarity toward conationals that transforms them into national states or "shared communities of fate."[56] As early as the 18th century, Johann Gottfried Herder, the German Romantic philosopher, considered a national community as natural as the family community: "Nature raises families; the most natural state is therefore also one people, with one national character. Through the millennia, this national character is maintained within a people and can be developed most naturally if its native prince so desires, for a people is as much a plant of nature as a family, only with more branches."[57] This sense of belonging to and solidarity with the nation is extraordinarily relevant to the modern political world, both because such narratives of national belonging ultimately legitimate the use of state power and because they legitimate the claims of rebels to oppose state power and pursue self-determination.

Together, nations and states constitute our contemporary global order to such a degree that they are often found in such hyphenated terms as "nation-state" and "state-nation."[58] It is not for nothing that most sovereign states have founding myths and museums narrating *national* stories; orchestras, holidays and libraries celebrating *national* cultures or heroes; and *national* armies protecting *national* borders. Constitutive stories of nationhood remain such a potent political force that politicians often hark back to them to portray policies as being in the *national* interest. Relations between states are often referred to in terms of inter*national* relations, and when states came together to form associations of mutual benefit, these were named the "League of Nations" and "United Nations" consecutively.[59] Political leaders even conflate states with nations. In his last speech at the UN, former US President Barack Obama said, "Just as we benefit by combatting inequality within our *countries,* I believe advanced economies still need to do more to close the gap between rich and poor *nations* around the globe."[60]

Yet despite the prominence of the nation as a relevant concept in contemporary political developments, no scholarship to our knowledge has advanced a systematic discussion of nationalism's dimensions. This stands in marked contrast to the scholarly debates on democracy, in which scholars have amply parsed major definitions and have established research projects (Freedom House, Polity V, and V-Dem) to conceptualize and track its multiple

---

[56] Rhodes 2019, chapter 3; Tamir 2019a.   [57] Herder 2004: 128.

[58] For a conceptual distinction in terms of whether the identity or the political project predominates, see Stepan et al. 2011.

[59] Connor 1978.

[60] President Obama's Final Address to the United Nations General Assembly delivered on September 20, 2016, New York,. Available here: www.americanrhetoric.com/speeches/barack obama/barackobamaunitednations71.htm. Emphasis added.

dimensions.[61] Providing an improved conceptual terrain for nationalism is essential to assessing its causes and consequences because any conclusions about nationalism will hinge crucially upon its definition. A paucity of conceptual clarity surrounding nationalism stems partly from the fact that the study of nationalism spans every conceivable methodological approach and a broad range of disciplines, including political science, history, philosophy, psychology, anthropology, and sociology.

We aim for this Element to serve as a stepping stone toward greater conceptual consistency and clarity. The remainder of this section begins this discussion *first* by synthesizing the major historical debates about where and why nationalism emerged, *second* by providing key definitions of nations and nationalism, and *third* by distinguishing nationalism from other ideologies and related concepts.

2.1 How Did Nations and Nationalism Come About?

Because few political creeds are as widely accepted and celebrated as that of national self-determination, one might forget that the very idea is a recent chapter in human history. As late as early twentieth-century Europe, the ruling elites of an empire or a city-state would have been alien to their subjects. Much as the Russian nobility in Tolstoy's *War and Peace* spoke a language not understood by most of their subjects, emperors and kings ruled over people who often did not speak the same language, sometimes did not practice the same religion, and occasionally did not even inhabit the same continent. Kings and queens legitimated their rule over peoples not by a sense of shared solidarity but by divine right and/or coercion. For most of human history, legitimate rule did not presuppose even a minimum degree of cultural similarity between rulers and subjects.

Early seeds of the global drive toward self-rule can be found in enlightenment thinkers who criticized absolute monarchies and the feudal social orders of Europe that dated from the late Middle Ages. While both Christian and Muslim thinkers in the Middle Ages argued that the ruler should be from the same religion of the ruled, ideas that government should rule in the name of *a people* and in their interest were catapulted into global prominence by the nearly contemporaneous American and French revolutions. Alexis de Tocqueville wrote in *Democracy in America* that the essential core of the new American political experiment was a public commitment to equality among its citizens, limited though it was by gender and race. Written for a European audience,

---

[61] For more see, https://freedomhouse.org/reports, www.systemicpeace.org/polityproject.html, www.v-dem.net/.

Tocqueville's writings were avidly read as a blueprint for what future European societies could become, thus playing an important part disseminating new ideas of what a society of equals could look like. The idea that alien rule broadly lacked legitimacy proliferated around the same time.[62]

While such changing ideational currents altered perceptions of possible political orders, so too did the changes in social and economic structures that scholars have broadly termed "modernization." *Modernist* scholars emphasize that nationalism only became possible amidst such tectonic social changes as industrialization, urbanization, mass education, communication, transportation, and the emergence of the modern state. Modernists emphasize alternate sets of causal pathways by which such dislocation spurred on the emergence and spread of nationalism. Urbanization and the new possibilities it created for communicating with large numbers of new people is one such causal pathway. The philosopher Jürgen Habermas describes the growth of a public sphere in seventeenth and eighteenth-century Europe to urban locales such as coffee houses: "The 'town' was the life centre of civil society not only economically; in cultural-political contrast to the court, it designated exactly an early public sphere in the world of letters whose institutions were the coffee houses, the salons, and the *Tischgesellschaften* (table societies)."[63] These developments formed critical antecedents for what Karl Deutsch discussed as social mobilization and social communication that ultimately led to the development of national communities. According to Deutsch, nationalism emerged from urbanization because "[m]embership in a people essentially consists in wide complementarity of social communication. It consists in the ability to communicate more effectively, and over a wider range of subjects, with members of one large group than with outsiders."[64]

Other modernist scholars place greater emphasis upon industrialization's need for an educated work force in germinating nationalism. Ernest Gellner argued that industrial society needed to equip workers with skills that could not be provided by families, churches, or the educational institutions of a traditional agrarian society. As peasants move to cities to participate in the new opportunities offered by industrialization, industrialists found they needed to train workers who were educated in a standardized idiom. Industrialists consequently lobbied governments to invest in public systems of education which political elites facilitated. According to such accounts, public education gradually composed and brought about a national imagined community.

Yet another vein of modernist scholarship proposes that print capitalism, with its attendant standardization of vernacular languages and drive for profit

---

[62] Hechter 2013.   [63] Habermas 1989: 30.   [64] Deutsch 1953: 97.

through mass readership, played a preeminent role in birthing nations and nationalism. In particular, Benedict Anderson argued that the desire of print capitalists to maximize profits by reaching as many readers as possible led to a standardization of language and provided the mechanism for the emergence of these new and imagined communities. The nation was created by a reading public that first transcended the boundaries of immediate local experience. Shared discourses and events narrated in books and daily newspapers shaped a common outlook: "What the eye is to the lover – that particular, ordinary eye he or she is born with – language –whatever language history has made his or her mother tongue – is to the patriot. Through that language, encountered at mother's knee and parted with only at the grave, pasts are restored, fellowships are imagined, and futures dreamed."[65] Taken as a whole, modernist scholars argue that nationalism was a by-product of the forces of modernization and, thus, individuals became members of a nation by participating in the modernization of their societies.

By contrast, *perennialist* scholars posited that nations are simply a modern veneer upon a form of solidarity that has always or perennially existed. All nations, such scholars argue, build upon some form of group solidarity that *always* or perennially derived from preexisting genetic, linguistic, religious, territorial, or kinship ties.[66] Such ties existed prior to the advent of modernity,[67] with some especially singling out religion as an especially important building block for nationalism.[68] Perennialist scholars were inspired by, but distinct from, German Romantics (which are often seen perhaps mistakenly as representing a primordialist view), who viewed nations as age-old entities awaiting awakening. Such definitions of the nation drew heavily from European experiences with the emergence of nations and were epitomized in the Warwick debates over the origins of the nation between Ernest Gellner and Anthony Smith.

Smith contended that there is such deep continuity between ancient cultures and ethnic communities on the one hand, and modern nation-states on the other, that they are inseparable. All nations and nationalisms, Smith argued, are ultimately ethnic: "History is no sweetshop in which its children may 'pick and mix' .... The challenge for scholars as well as nations is to represent the relationship of ethnic past to modern nation more accurately and convincingly." [69]

Gellner (2006) countered that nations do not always have ethnic pasts; therefore, ethnic building blocks are neither necessary nor sufficient for nations to emerge. Estonians, for example, possessed no ethnic consciousness nor even a name for themselves at the start of the nineteenth century, but they created

---

[65] Anderson 1983: 154.   [66] Smith 1986, 1991, 1998: 145–153, 223.
[67] Shils 1957; Geertz 1963; Smith 1986, 1991; Gorski 2000.   [68] Hastings 1997; Gorski 2003.
[69] Smith 1995: 18.

a nation, national consciousness, and a nation-state within 100 years. Consequently, though nations may reflect cultural continuities with premodern ethnic sensibilities, this relationship is contingent and inessential.

While deliberations between modernists and perennialists over nationalism's origins have not entirely disappeared,[70] contemporary research largely substantiates the claims of modernists. Presumed primordial commonalities of modern nations have been often found to be inconsistent with empirical realities within states and/or citizen's conceptualization of national identity. Scholarship has identified how such forces as industrialization, urbanization, mass communication, education, anti-colonialism, and global diffusion both evoked and shaped nationalism.[71] But, scholarship emphasizing the primordial origins of nations can neither account for changes in national belonging over time nor the timing of "national awakenings."[72]

In the words of Liah Greenfeld, nationalism is the *sine qua non* feature of modern societies.[73] Once a sense of shared identity emerged, it was reinforced by the community of nation-states and shaped the possibilities of future politics. As Deutsch argued, "Governments can modify communities, and they can make communities in rare and favorable situations; but on the whole it is the communities which make governments, or rather, it is the distribution of communities at any one time which both offers and limits the opportunities for governments to consolidate and extend their power."[74]

In sum, much contemporary political science scholarship understands the nation as emerging from a contingent, contextually specific, and still-evolving macro-historical process of identification with the state rather than as an entity with fixed relevance or meaning.[75] Rational-choice explanations of nationalism argue that nations are a coordinated set of beliefs about their cultural identities whose representatives can claim ownership of a state and that the benefits of coordination explain the stickiness of these national identities.[76] Yet most people are born into the citizenship of a nation-state and tend to experience it as part of the natural political order.

While a broad scholarly consensus that the nation is a recent and imagined identity dominates political science, it is worth remembering that a sense of the nation as an ancient community pervades both popular discourse around nationalism as well as sociological and historical accounts of nations. This is because making and commemorating history is an essential exercise in making nations.

---

[70] Breuilly 2013; Gat 2013; Malešević 2013; Coakley 2017.
[71] Deutsch 1953, 1961, 1969; Weber 1976; Anderson 1983; Hobsbawm and Ranger 1983; Gellner 2006; Lawrence 2013; Darden and Mylonas 2016.
[72] Renan 1882; Gellner 2006; Anderson 1983; Laitin 2007; Brubaker 1996.
[73] Greenfeld 1992.   [74] Deutsch 1953, 79.   [75] Brubaker 1996, 2004.   [76] Laitin 2007.

As one of the earliest scholars of nationalism Ernest Renan wrote, "The nation, like the individual, is the outcome of a long past of efforts, sacrifices, and devotion. Of all cults, that of the ancestors is the most legitimate: our ancestors have made us who we are. A heroic past with great men and glory is the social capital upon which the national idea rests." [77]

2.2 Definitions

Nations and the nationalisms that celebrate them vary tremendously because these nations are built with blocks of assorted types and shapes. Members of a nation typically share one or more of the key family resemblances of shared language, religion, ethnicity, or civic ideals, and – if they have managed to achieve sovereignty – geographical borders. But the central characteristics for membership in a national community in one case may be irrelevant in another case. Some national communities are not built around a common language (e.g., Switzerland, India), a shared religion (e.g., Nigeria, Canada), an homogenous ethnic core (e.g., United States, Brazil, South Africa), or even contiguous geographical borders (e.g., Indonesia, New Zealand, Japan, and the Philippines). Because nations have a Wittgenstein-like "family resemblance" in which no one characteristic is essential,[78] definitions of nations and national-ism are necessarily broad.

In our framework, a nation is:

(1) *A type of social identity.*

(2) *That aspires to some degree of political self-rule over a distinct territory.*

Philosophers, political scientists, and sociologists have articulated nearly as many definitions of the 'nation' as there are nations, leading to a considerable degree of conceptual confusion. Scholars generally agree that the nation is a type of constructed social *identity* or a social category that individuals qualify for by virtue of certain practices, beliefs, and/or inheritable attributes. As we discussed above, most contemporary scholars understand the nation to be imagined (*mod-ernists/constructivists*), though some scholars argue that nations or proto-nations existed prior to the advent of modernity *(perennialists)* while even fewer believe that modern nations are built upon inheritable ethnic traits that emerged many centuries ago and have been durable ever since *(primordialists)*.

All individuals possess multiple, nested identities.[79] Professions, localities, families, local associations, sexual orientations, race, and ethnicity are all forms of identity. Yet the existence of an identity does not automatically translate into

---

[77] Renan 1882: 153.   [78] Wittgenstein 2001(1953).   [79] Allport et al. 1954.

either consciousness of that identity, much less its use as the basis for sustained political action. Groups of peoples across the United Kingdom, Ireland, France, and Spain have Celtic origins. But this identity has not translated into a developed awareness of this identity, much less coordinated political action on that basis. This Celtic identity is believed to be descent-based, thus ethnic, but it does not necessarily involve a claim for autonomy or independence.

In contrast, a nation is a social identity premised upon *both* group self-awareness as well as some pursuit of self-rule and sovereignty over a distinct territory. What distinguishes the nation as an identity from other forms of group solidarity is thus that it *definitionally* entails a desire for self-rule, wherein a people cares enough about that identity to aspire to be ruled by those like themselves.[80]

As we discussed earlier, for a sentiment/identity to qualify as nationalism/ nationalist, it *must* include institutionalized political organization – at least by a significant segment of elites or members of a community – aspiring for sovereignty over a particular territory. It is in this way that a nation is distinct from other social identities such as castes, clans, kinship groups, or tribes.[81] As the turbulent history of coexistence of the four nations – England, Northern Ireland, Scotland, and Wales – within the United Kingdom shows, the drive for self-rule may fluctuate and at times shy away from full-blown political sovereignty.

Intellectuals and scholars have argued that a multitude of attributes, practices, and beliefs may define a nation. Founding national narratives have been mapped onto inheritable physical traits, ethnic affinities, racial categories, language, geography, religious doctrine, or shared culture. Some of the earliest thinkers of nations and national belonging, such as the German Romantic philosopher Johann Gottfried Herder, wrote that national communities were distinguishable through objective, shared attributes, in particular language.[82] Johann Gottlieb Fichte (1762–1814) whose writings developed in reaction to the nineteenth-century occupation of German territories by Napoleon's forces, argued that language was a natural phenomenon. These philosophers stipulated that a shared language defined the natural boundaries of a *Volk* – which loosely translates to both people and nation in English. While scholars have long argued that ethnicity, race, religion, geography, culture or language are all core building blocks for a nation, contemporary empirical scholarship shows that none of these conditions are either sufficient or necessary for

---

[80] However, the likelihood of these feelings turning into full-fledged nationalism is also driven by prior structural factors, such as the size and the related possibility of economic self-sufficiency. We thank Professor Atul Kohli for clarifying this point.

[81] Mylonas and Pasha, unpublished manuscript.   [82] Herder 2004; Fichte 2008.

a nation to exist. We thus argue that nationalism should be conceptually delinked from ethnicity.

Nationalism – or the celebration of the nation – entails:

1. *The intersubjective recognition of an imagined community of people as a locus of loyalty and solidarity,*

2. *The desire for some degree of self-rule over a distinct territory, and*

3. *A repertoire of symbols and practices that embody and celebrate that imagined community, ranging from monuments and museums to festivals and holidays.*

"Nationalism" has *three* defining elements. The *first defining element* of nationalism is the intersubjective recognition of a community of individuals who conceive of themselves as a single people in the absence of face-to-face interaction.[83] For much of history, humans lived in communities where they physically encountered each member. Such communities – typically several hundred people – were not imagined but witnessed and tangibly experienced. The evolution of larger communities of solidarity and cooperation was arguably the single most important ingredient to the success of human societies. When stories of common belonging emerged, they enabled human cooperation to unfold to an unprecedented degree among much larger groups, including among individuals who they would never physically meet.[84] While Benedict Anderson's pithy "imagined community" is the most well-known description of a nation, other scholars of nationalism have echoed that the nation is similarly a "daily plebiscite," and nationalism an "invented tradition" or a "lie that binds."[85] In articulating these definitions, most scholars agree that nationalism involves an enormously consequential but ultimately imagined community as a locus of loyalty and solidarity.

A *second defining element* of a nationalism is a conscious and articulated desire for self-rule and political sovereignty over a distinct territory – at least by a significant segment of elites or members of an imagined community.[86] As Hegel already wrote in the late 1820s, "in the existence of a people, the substantial purpose is to be a state, and to maintain itself as such."[87] Yet this sense of national belonging does not cleanly map onto

---

[83] Anderson 1983.   [84] Harari 2014; Veyne 1988.

[85] Renan 1882; Hobsbawm and Ranger 1983; Appiah 2018.

[86] Demands limited to cultural recognition or minority rights does not fall under our definition of nationalism unless they are part of a broader gradual strategy of escalating to demands for self-rule over a particular territory.

[87] Quoted from Mead 1882: 196, also found in Hegel 1830.

borders recognized by the United Nations. In some internationally sovereign states such as Japan, citizens are largely understood to be members of a single national community. But some sovereign states contain several different nations, and some sub-national identities can rank higher in peoples' daily plebiscites or even be antagonistic to the identity associated with the political unit ultimately possessing sovereignty.[88]

Particularly in such contexts, it becomes important to draw analytical distinctions between *states* and *nations* and to understand the complex interactions between national and sub-national identities. For instance, the United Kingdom, a sovereign state with the power to take its own foreign policy and monetary decisions, is comprised of four nations: Wales, Northern Ireland, Scotland, and England. A clear majority of Scotland's residents today identify themselves as strongly Scottish and some of them also strongly British, though Scots on average feel less British than do the English.[89] A latent, but recently active, claim to self-rule by significant sections of Scots places this identity squarely into the nationalism category.

Moreover, governing elites of some states such as Armenia, Israel, Hungary, and India believe that important parts of their national community live outside of their current state borders. Thus, nationalism is defined *both* by large-scale solidarity and a sentiment "aimed at creating, legitimating or challenging states."[90] As Ernest Gellner wrote, nationalism is above all "a political principle, which holds that the political and the national unit should be congruent."[91] Thus, nationalist movements may seek to achieve this congruence by trying to unify territories inhabited by people they perceive as conationals in more than one states or seeking self-determination for a segment of an existing state they consider their homeland.

A *third defining element* of nationalism – increasingly investigated by recent scholarship – is the implicit celebration of the nation through a repertoire of popular practices and symbols. A growing scholarship documents how a subliminal awareness of nationalism is seeded through ordinary *symbols* – from flags on public buildings, statues in public squares, and images on the national currency – and practices – from national holidays, the singing of songs to honor key national moments, or festivals that celebrate national heroes or cuisines.[92] And even state institutions, far from remaining impersonal, can often acquire emotive and symbolic meaning that motivates political action.[93] Nationalism thus also includes the "'nation'-oriented idioms, practices, and

---

[88] Rutland and Cinnirella 2010.   [89] www.bbc.co.uk/news/uk-scotland-44208691.
[90] Marx 2005: 6.   [91] Gellner 2006: 1.   [92] Billig 1995.   [93] Basta 2021; Lenton 2021.

possibilities that are continuously available or 'endemic' in modern cultural and political life."[94]

Nationalism is thus a more capacious and political concept than citizenship, which is primarily a legal concept. The "right to nationality" (here denoting legal citizenship) was enshrined in the 1948 Universal Declaration of Human Rights as one of thirty inalienable rights. Yet there is no doubt that nationalism is bound up with state power and citizenship. As Hannah Arendt famously suggested, the "right to have rights" presupposes a political entity willing to enforce such rights – and the system of nation-states was probably the most likely to protect such rights.

Elites and everyday people identifying with the Kurdish national self-determination movement reside and have citizenship in several countries including Turkey, Iraq, Iran, and Syria.[95] Despite the wide variation in terms of their treatment in each country, the Kurdish case exemplifies the distinction between national identity and citizenship. Moving to a case from Southeast Asia, in 1989 a new government changed the official English-language name of the country from the Union of Burma to the Union of Myanmar, keeping it intact in Burmese as "Myanma pyi." The government's claim was that this move would make the country more inclusive toward Indigenous peoples. But several ethnic minorities in the country rejected the renaming arguing that "Myanmar" only represented the Burmese majority ethnic group, accusing the government of assimilationist intent aiming at Myanmarization of all groups in the country (Garrity 2022: 316). In 1990s, the newly renamed Myanmar government documented 135 "national ethnic races" that were considered to be "pure-blooded nationals" and thus assimilable. Some of these groups, such as the Karen or Kachin fit our definition of a national movement, but they also qualified as citizens of Myanmar. This demonstrates that these concepts of nationality and citizenship are analytically distinct.

In the case of the Rohingya, they were not included in the list of "national ethnic races" and the Myanmar government practically denied Rohingya's' citizenship rights since 1982. More recently, a United Nations fact-finding mission stated: "The Rohingya are in a continuing situation of severe, systemic, and institutionalized oppression from birth to death. The cornerstone and symbol of this system is their complete lack of legal status, including the denial of citizenship."[96] The Rohingya are part of a growing global community of

---

[94] Brubaker 2004: 10. [95] Jwaideh 2006; Romano 2006.
[96] www.ohchr.org/EN/HRBodies/HRC/Pages/NewsDetail.aspx?NewsID=23575&LangID=E. .

stateless individuals around the globe, including for example, the Palestinians, the Bidoon people, or the Nubians.[97]

Nationalism's three defining features are thus (1) the intersubjective recognition and celebration of an imagined community of people as a locus of loyalty and solidarity; (2) the pursuit of self-rule on the basis of that identity; and, (3) a set of everyday cultural practices or symbols that can instantiate or thicken a sense of belonging to the nation. But scholars also agree that nationalism often remains a *thin* identity that can – and has been – combined with a range of other ideologies such as liberalism, illiberalism, socialism, capitalism, multiculturalism, populism, religion, and racism.

2.3 How Nationalism Relates to Other -isms

Public discourse makes a common distinction between *patriotism* and nationalism that, while empirically demonstrable, remains unstable. Patriotism has much older genealogy than nationalism, often taken to describe a person's positive attachment, affection, and willingness to sacrifice for a particular territory considered to be their homeland, which could be an empire or city-state as well as a nation-state.[98] Discussions of patriotism are found in some of the earliest works of the Ancient literature: Hector, leader of the Trojans in the Trojan War, urges Polydamas in Book 12 of Homer's *Iliad*,: "Fight for your country – that is the best, the only omen."[99] A citizen of a Greek city-state, like Hector, but equally a member of the Ottoman empire could both be patriots, though their *terra patria* assumed fundamentally different political forms. Nationalism, by contrast, is defined as political loyalty to a people forming a national community specifically.

The distinction between good forms of nationalism ("patriotism") and bad forms of nationalism ("nationalism") that is popular in everyday political discourse is empirically problematic. All nationalisms harness the potential for exclusion, since all groups define themselves, at least in part, against "out-groups." Michael Walzer writes that "admission and exclusion are at the core of communal independence. They suggest the deepest meaning of self-determination. Without them, there could not be communities of character, historically stable, ongoing associations of men and women with some special commitment to one another and some special sense of their common life." [100] All meaningful groups draw boundaries to exclude

---

[97] Siegelberg 2020.
[98] Nathanson 1993: 34–35. For discussions of classical patriotism before the advent of nationalism, see Viroli 1995.
[99] Professor George Th. Mavrogordatos, personal communication. Also see Mavrogordatos 2020.
[100] Walzer 1983: 62.

outsiders. But this does not mean that the types, extent, and principled bases of nationalisms are irrelevant.

Popular discourse as well as scholarly works draw distinctions between nationalism and patriotism not in terms of their core focus–people or land, respectively–but in terms of whether individuals possess a simple pride in nation that *does not* belittle foreign nations (patriotism) and a pride in nation that *does* inherently invoke superiority toward other nations (chauvinistic nationalism). Many scholars have tried to empirically distinguish between these two phenomena, with patriotism invariably characterized by rationality, constitutionalism, and principles; while nationalism being associated with irrational ethnic attachments, bellicosity, and fanaticism.[101]

Yet such a conceptual distinction between patriotism and nationalism is often empirically problematic and stems from an uncritical acceptance of conceptual distinctions such as those initially drawn by Hans Kohn. Positive evaluations of national pride (patriotism) are too often aligned with the national identity of authors themselves. For instance, the American political scientist Walker Connor correctly characterizes the national narratives of Mao Zedong in China and Adolf Hitler in Germany as "nationalist" but describes American nationalism as "patriotic." Similarly, the German philosopher Jürgen Habermas draws clear distinctions between Germany's pre–World War II nationalism and Germany's post–World War II *Verfassungspatriotismus* (constitutional patriotism). Hannah Arendt (1963) argues that the main difference between the French and American Revolutions is that political authority in the former was derived from the nation that assumed the rule of the king, whereas in the US authority was derived from loyalty to the institutions and therefore the latter succeeded.

Even when scholars have used survey data to substantiate these distinctions between nationalism and patriotism empirically, we find similar trends.[102] For example, Kosterman and Feshbach (1989) have written one of the most cited pieces of empirical work investigating this distinction. But American patriotism *and* nationalism are highly correlated with each other. Moreover, survey research has also shown that priming, especially through the nature of the comparison group, affects whether so called patriotism or nationalism is elicited.[103] As Li and Brewer write: "As two different sides of the same coin, it is possible that 'love of nation' can be associated with benign patriotic attitudes under some circumstances *or* with more malign nationalistic attitudes in other circumstances, within the same

---

[101] Snyder 1976; Connor 1972, 1994; Janowitz 1983; Habermas 1996.

[102] Kosterman and Feshbach 1989; Blank and Schmidt 2003.

[103] Hinkle and Brown 1990; Billig 1995; Mummendey, Klink and Brown 2001; Li and Brewer 2004.

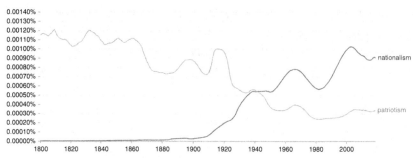

Figure 3 Frequency of "nationalism" and "patriotism" in books, 1800 to 2019

individual."[104] It is thus doubtful whether scholars can draw sharp, durable distinctions between the two concepts.[105] It may well be that a distinction between patriotism and nationalism is simply a phenomenon with two faces, like the Roman god Janus. Scholarly conceptions of identity and attachment to nation may simply have developed independently over time and which have not been critically examined vis-à-vis one another, as Figure 3 suggests. Indeed, survey research substantiating an empirical distinction between nationalism and patriotism typically relies upon cross-sectional data at one moment in time and rarely examines whether the patriotism/nationalism distinction remains stable over time.

Nationalism and *liberalism* both have featured prominently in late eighteenth-century movements for freedom and justice, especially the self-determination movements overthrowing absolute monarchies in the wake of the American and French Revolutions and the national movements overthrowing racially and economically exploitative colonial regimes. Several leaders of nationalist movements drew on liberal ideas of self-determination, constitutional government, and individual liberty to justify their struggles against *anciens régimes* such as the Ottoman and Spanish empires. But while liberalism focuses on the rights of individuals – be these rights, freedom, or equality[106] – nationalism definitionally prioritizes group rights such as the defense of the national interest, the right to national health care, or the protection of borders.[107]

What do communists make of nationalism?[108] While nationalist ideology emphasizes horizontal identity boundaries between different national groups, communism emphasizes the vertical economic boundaries between the

---

[104] Li and Brewer 2004: 728. Emphasis in original.
[105] For an excellent discussion of their problematic conclusions, see Billig (1995): 57–58. Also, Canovan (2000).
[106] Rawls 1993; Berlin 1969. For a recent discussion of nationalism and liberalism, see Fukuyama 2022.
[107] Taylor 1992; Tamir 1993; Herder 2004; Mounk 2022.   [108] Connor 1984.

"proletariat" and the "bourgeoisie" irrespective of horizontal national boundaries. Marxists and Leninists have argued that "[n]ationalism was mainly a device of the bourgeoisie for identifying their class interests as the interests of the entire society" and that nationalism would eventually disappear as a political force.[109] In Lenin's "strategic Marxist" writings, nationalism was seen as necessary in the period prior to the proletarian revolution but reactionary in the postrevolutionary period.[110] National bourgeois revolutions were necessary in the sense that they helped overthrow feudal regimes and move societies into the industrial revolution. Because of its association with a specific stage in economic development, "nationalism could be progressive or reactionary, depending upon the level of society. At a feudal or semifeudal stage, it is progressive, but at a stage of developed capitalism it is counterrevolutionary."[111]

Nationalism's definitional emphasis upon the horizontal relationships between conationals differs from *populism's* definitional emphasis upon the vertical antagonism between elites and the rest of the population.[112] In recent decades, nationalism has often been conflated with populism, making this a particularly important distinction.[113] Nationalism centralizes the legitimacy of a *horizontal* boundary between citizen in-groups and foreigner out-groups, while populism centralizes a *vertical* boundary between a corrupt parasitic elite and a genuine and untainted "people" who are the source of democratic legitimacy. Populism thus "considers society to be ultimately separated into two homogeneous and antagonistic groups, 'the pure people' versus 'the corrupt elite', and which argues that politics should be an expression of the *volonté générale* (general will) of the people."[114] Thus, while these two -isms can be empirically combined and often are in the case of contemporary political movements, they remain analytically distinct.

Nationalism is not destined to lead to *fascism* because not all varieties of nationalism require a total surrender of other identities and values to an organic national community. To be sure, extreme forms of nationalism can – and have – morphed into fascism. But fascism is a particular anti-liberal and anti-communist form of nationalism where a dictator establishes a totalitarian regime and subjugates individual rights, desires, or differences to his/her vision of the national organic community.

And finally, scholars have recently explored whether nationalism can be compatible with *cosmopolitanism* – the view that "one's primary moral obligations are directed to all human beings (regardless of geographical or cultural distance), and political arrangements should faithfully reflect this universal

---

[109] Connor 1984: 7.   [110] Connor 1984: xiii.   [111] Connor 1984: 7.

[112] For a useful commentary on Mudde's (2004) definition of populism see Brubaker (2017) where he disentangles populism into different types of rhetorical devices and approaches.

[113] Often referred to as the "new nationalism."   [114] Mudde 2004: 543.

moral obligation (in the form of supra-statist arrangements that take precedence over nation-states)."[115] There is little agreement on these questions. While some argue that there is a structural tension between cosmopolitanism and nationalism that the ongoing migration "crises" in the European Union have underscored,[116] others suggest that there is no fundamental tension between cosmopolitanism and nationalism, much in the way that there is not necessarily a contradiction between feeling attached to New York City and feeling attached to the United States.[117] This latter view appears to be empirically supported by survey research. For example, the recent World Values Survey found that those who strongly agreed with the statement "I see myself as a world citizen" were *more* likely to also strongly affirm their sense of belonging to their nation, which accords with research supporting that the supranational European identity and nation-state identities coexist effortlessly in a "marble cake" fashion.[118] Regardless, the source of the latent tension between nationalism and cosmopolitanism is a disagreement about to *whom* we owe *what* moral obligations, especially when our obligations collide; thus, demonstrating that people can *often* identify with both conationals and fellow humans neither confirms nor denies this fundamental tension.

3 Does a Nation Exist?

> "No community is natural but no community is uncontested either."
> Smith (2003)

Nationalism is definitionally oriented toward aspiring, creating, legitimating, and challenging states – and thus presumes that the world should be divided into nation-states.[119] But not all national communities have the same levels of national cohesion – either at the elite or at popular levels. Elite and popular fragmentation, refer to the degree of agreement among the main political elites and/or the population, within a territory or movement, over the definition of the nation.[120] Scholars have shown that the degree of elite and popular fragmentation, especially at nation-founding moments, varies and moreover, that this variance crucially shapes political outcomes ranging from violence, public goods provision, public attitudes, and the attraction of investment. In Taiwan for example, post–World War II KMT elites were largely unified in their "One China narrative" while the population who had resided on the island before KMT's arrival in 1949 became skeptical about its sinicization efforts over time.[121]

---

[115] Miscevic 2018.   [116] Krastev 2017.   [117] Appiah 2018.   [118] Risse 2004; Bayram 2019.
[119] Smith 2003; Malešević 2019.   [120] Shevel 2011.
[121] We thank Eun A Jo for her elaboration of this point. See also Corcuff and Edmundson (2002) and Jo (forthcoming).

3.1 Elite Fragmentation

The first dimension along which nationalism varies is *elite fragmentation* – or the degree of agreement among the main political elites within a territory (or a national movement) over the definition of the nation.[122] Political elites can disagree vehemently over the national narrative, denoting a high degree of fragmentation.[123] Or the elites can be almost entirely united over the national narrative, denoting low fragmentation. To the extent that one identifiable rendition of the narrative gains widespread elite acceptance, it can be said to be dominant.[124]

Classical scholarship on nationalism, concerned primarily with the *origins* of the first national states and nations, heavily focused upon Europe. Scholars argued that, with important exceptions such as Germany, states emerged before nations. In fact, only those states which were effective at fighting wars survived. Only later did elites leading surviving states attempt to mold individuals into citizens[125] while states with weak war-making capacity were absorbed or conquered by those with strong war-making capacity. Charles Tilly notably summarized this thesis that "war made the state and the state made war."[126] Though war-making is still understood to be crucial to state-making, and thus nation-making in Europe,[127] this process was less relevant to state- and nation-making beyond Europe.

Nonetheless, the processes of state-formation were similarly elite-led beyond Europe. Legions of new states were established in the last two centuries through imperial collapse, secessionist movements and anti-colonial movements. But whereas European states were built to win battles, most states beyond Europe were built through quite different processes. Latin American states were largely created to effectively pursue markets, while state boundaries in Africa and South Asia were often drawn by the pens of distant imperial rulers.[128] In the vast majority of these new states, the process of state-building was intimately bound up with Indigenous elites' pursuit of power through anti-colonial independence movements. These nascent national communities were also typically led by Indigenous, well-educated elites claiming to represent a fledging nation.[129] Where and when such elites were successful in claiming to represent a nation,

---

[122] Shevel 2011. [123] Mavrogordatos 1983, 2020. [124] Tudor 2013.

[125] For example, Weber (1976) details how elites turned "Peasants into Frenchmen."

[126] Tilly 1975: 42. Important critiques of Tilly's bellicist account include Spruyt (1994) and Grzymala-Busse (2020).

[127] Posen 1993; Darden and Mylonas 2016.

[128] For arguments about the creation of Latin America, see Centeno 2002 and Mazucca 2021. For sub-Saharan Africa, see Herbst 2000. For Asia, see Wang 2005.

[129] Gellner 2006; Lawrence 2013; Tudor 2013.

the founding national narratives tended to "settle" into popular imagination through the standardization of language, through school teachings about "we the people,"[130] and through the omnipresent culture repertoire of flags, songs, and cultural celebrations that Michael Billig terms "banal nationalism."[131] Once nationalisms settled, they were difficult to change, except in "unsettled" times.[132]

Scholarship spanning three time periods and four countries – eighteenth-century United States, nineteenth-century France and twenty-first-century Pakistan and India – illustrates how elites can be more or less fragmented. American elites were deeply fragmented around the question of whether black people were to count as citizens from the founding of the nation.[133] Like elsewhere in the world, the anti-colonial struggle against British imperialism was a kind of glue that soldered together disparate groups of peoples. Because the most powerful elites in that society were British descendants seeking religious freedoms, the country's statement of founding principles, its declaration of independence and later its constitution, afforded a central place to religious freedom. Like in other colonial contexts at the time, elites agreed that Native Americans, Black Americans, and women were not considered full citizens of the nation. Yet southern elites of sub-national states, which relied heavily upon slave labor to run its agricultural economy, objected strenuously to the counting of slaves as people in its population count, which also determined its share of tax burden. This was neither merely a technical nor economic matter – it was a matter of who was counted among "we the people" – the very three opening words of the American constitution. Divisions between southern elites, committed to plantation agriculture, and northern elites, relying on manufacturing and industrial production, as to whether and to what degree that "people" should include Black Americans was the single most important political divide during the time that the American republic was founded.[134]

American elites' fragmentation over race, which defined the nation at its founding, was institutionalized in party-based power struggles between elites. And the fragmentation in elite narratives continues to define American politics through to the present day, forming the most enduring political divide in American history and the single most important influence upon some of the most important events in American history – the Civil War in the nineteenth century, the civil rights movement in the twentieth century, and the Black Lives Matter movement in the twenty-first century.[135]

---

[130] For an excellent account of how national schooling operated in French Catalonia versus Spanish Catalonia, see Balcells 2013. For a general account of the effects of schooling on linguistic homogeneity, see Darden and Mylonas 2016.
[131] Billig 1995.   [132] Aktürk 2012; Bonikowski 2016.   [133] Lipset 1963.   [134] Smith 1997.
[135] Wilkerson 2020; Woodly 2021.

French elites were much less divided over their narrative of their nation throughout this same time period.

> From the time of the Revolution in 1789 to the beginning of the Fifth Republic, the French were able to accommodate to relatively abrupt changes of regime in part because there was *broad agreement* about the nature of French national identity. . . .For there was a common religion, a common culture, a (more or less) common language that united most of the inhabitants of France.[136]

As Eugene Weber has argued, it was primarily French elites in charge of the French state who were united, as the French countryside reflected an incredibly diverse fabric with little in the way of shared traditions and even dialects. "Villages hated each other from time immemorial, and all hated the gentlemen of the bourgeoisie."[137]

Elite unity around narratives of the nation varied among postcolonial states. Pakistani elites were highly fragmented as to their understanding of the nation at the country's inception. Muslim elites across British colonial India were able to come together in a nationalist movement to assert the right to Pakistan by mobilizing on the basis of Islam in the decade before independence. However, once the state was created and the shared religious identity could be taken for granted, other cleavages immediately began to emerge among elites, particularly between the Punjabi-speaking *pir*-landlord elites of West Pakistan and the more numerous Bengali-speaking peasant cultivators of East Pakistan. Because these newer cleavages of language, class, and culture overlapped with geography, elites fragmented along linguistic and regional cleavages to such a degree that such fragmentation caused regime instability in the immediate aftermath of independence.[138] As Figure 4 shows, elite fragmentation around competing narratives of the nation along two questions – whether Islam should define the nation and what languages should be the official ones – was the chief cause, two and a half decades later, of Pakistan's breakup into the sovereign successor states of Pakistan and Bangladesh.[139]

By contrast, the elites leading India's national community were far more unified, in part because their nationalist movement, active for three decades before independence, was substantially older and more ideologically cohesive and disciplined. Though elite fragmentation about the national narrative did exist and can be traced to foundational understandings of the role of the state in the economy and society upon colonial independence, they were largely contained within what Ranji Kothari called the "Congress system."[140]

---

[136] Safran 1990: 56–57. Emphasis added.   [137] Weber 1976: 47.
[138] McGrath 1998; Tudor 2013; Jalal 2014.   [139] Sisson and Rose 1990, chapter 5.
[140] Kothari 1964; Chhibber and Verma 2018.

(a)

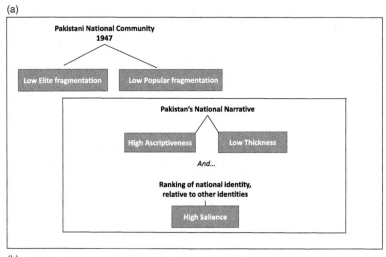

(b)

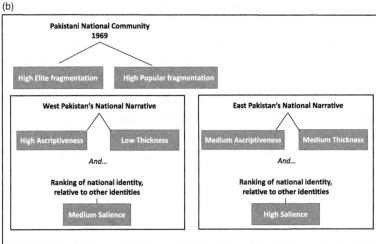

(c)

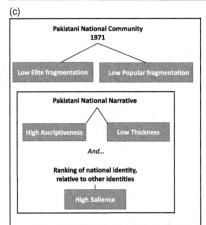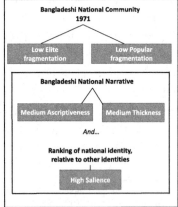

Figure 4 Elite and popular fragmentation

Specifically, anti-colonial Indian nationalism witnessed one major cleavage around the role of religion in defining the nation at the moment of independence. Hindu nationalism was juxtaposed with Nehruvian nationalism, at a time when most of the population was rural, illiterate, and mostly untouched by the forces of nationalism. Hindu nationalists emphasized the primacy of ethnoreligious attributes of belonging, specifying that the Indian nation was foremost instantiated by cultural dimensions, specifically the religion of almost three-quarters of the population (Hinduism). In the words of the Vinayak Damodar Sarvarkar, who founded the concept of *Hindutva* or Hindu nationalism in 1923, "[e]very person is a Hindu who regards and owns this Bharat Bhumi, this land from the Indus to the seas, as his Fatherland as well as Holyland, i.e. the land of the origin of his religion. Consequently, the so-called aboriginal or hill tribes also are Hindus because India is their Fatherland as well as their Holyland of whatever form of religion or worship they follow." According to this line of thought, religious minorities were converts who should recognize the cultural centrality of the Hindu religion in defining India.[141]

Elites espousing Nehruvian nationalism, named after India's first prime minister Jawaharlal Nehru, rejected Hinduism as the defining feature of the nation and instead embraced western conceptions of secularism and unity amidst diversity. Like many of the English-speaking elites educated in colonial institutions, Nehru felt that India was a secular state "which honours all faiths equally and gives them equal opportunities; that, as a state, it does not allow itself to be attached to one faith or religion, which then becomes the state religion. Where the great majority of people in a state belong to one religion, this fact alone may colour, to some extent, the cultural climate of that state. But nevertheless the state, as a state, can remain independent of any particular religion."[142] Economically, Nehruvian nationalism gave an expansive role to the state, focusing on the need for the state to spearhead industrialization and alleviate poverty.

Upon independence, Hindu nationalists' understanding of nationhood was profoundly delegitimised and Nehruvian nationalism gained widespread acceptance among early political elites. Elite cohesion over India's dominant narrative emerged both because a Congress led by Nehru took power and because the twin shocks of India's partition on the grounds of religion and Gandhi's assassination by a Hindu nationalist, which further

---

[141] For a nice overview of the dominant and official conceptions of the Indian nation and Hindu nationalism, see Varshney 1993.

[142] Gopal 1983: 330.

undermined Hindu nationalism. Thus, while elite understandings of the Indian nation did vary, and while these differences have remained fundamental political cleavages in Indian politics,[143] a secular conception of the Indian nation was broadly dominant among Indian elites up from the time of independence until the 1980s, during which time Indian elites were broadly united on what defined their nation.

The four abovementioned examples evidence how elites can be varyingly fragmented, both at the founding moment of their state and over time – with American and Pakistani elites more fragmented that their French and Indian counterparts over what defined their nations.[144] So where does elite fragmentation come from? Elite fragmentation often results from historically specific power struggles institutionalized in founding moment narratives, moments which often continue to shape contemporary politics in these countries. Both recent and older scholarship shows that there is nothing foreordained about how or why elites articulate particular national narratives – they are almost always constructed by elites for a range of instrumental and situational reasons.[145] For instance, much of what Mylonas and Radnitz (2022) call "fifth-column politics" involves elite attempts to redraw the boundaries of inclusion in society, especially in an attempt to divide their political opposition. Relatedly, Rogers Smith (2003) argues that leaders propose stories that resonate *and* make themselves central to the core group while clearly defining who is not a member. Rogers Brubaker's (1992) foundational work comparing understandings of nationhood in Germany versus France points to historical legacies of state-building. Germany's high level of elite fragmentation at the time of unification with federal features was ultimately resolved through the adoption of an ethnocultural definition of nation, while France's low level of elite fragmentation around a civic definition of the nation emerged because state centralization *preceded* the founding national moment.

Higher levels of external threat tend to play an important role in both unifying elites around national narratives and in incentivizing such elites to pursue nation-building policies.[146] Yet even when states invest strenuous efforts in consolidating social cohesion, sub-national groups sometimes form nationalist

---

[143] Chhibber and Verma 2018.

[144] Horowitz 1985; Lieberman 2003; Brubaker 2004; Posner 2005, 2017; Chandra 2012. Scholars such as Stein Rokkan, Martin Lipset, David Laitin, Kanchan Chandra, and Dan Posner, have tried to account for the origins of cleavage structures as well as their transformations.

[145] Brubaker 1992, 1996; Sewell 1996; Smith 1997, 2003; Laitin 1998; Wedeen 2008; Mylonas and Shelef 2014, 2017.

[146] Darden and Mylonas 2016.

movements aspiring to states of their own. Sometimes successfully so, as in the recent cases of peaceful partition in Czech Republic, Slovakia, and Montenegro, or violent secession in cases such as East Timor, Eritrea, Kosovo, and South Sudan.[147]

Mylonas and Shelef (2014) have shown that elite fragmentation of national communities can also occur within stateless national movements. In the same way that elite fragmentation has led to existing states to fragment into separate national communities and corresponding nation-states; stateless national movements can also fragment.

Tribes, religious groups, language communities, clans, and kinship groups existed long before modern understandings of nationhood emerged. Only a few of these cleavages became politically activated and even fewer ended up as the basis for a modern nation-state. But once elites called nations into being through narratives of belonging, the elite cleavages around those narratives became durable influences on nations' subsequent political trajectories. Though they do not necessarily term divides over national narratives "elite fragmentation," scholars have shown that the degree of agreement among the main political elites over the definition of the nation has causal relevance for a diverse range of outcomes such as race relations, state capacity, and democracy. For example, in South Africa, Brazil, and the United States, Anthony Marx (1998) argues that different levels of elite fragmentation around race in defining each nation accounts for the contemporary contours of race relations in these countries. Evan Lieberman (2003) similarly finds that a relatively cohesive vision of the national political community in South Africa – built by an elite united by a shared interest in maintaining institutionalized white supremacy – accounts for South Africa's historically progressive tax capacity, compared to Brazil whose elites were historically divided along questions of racial definitions of citizenship and were thus not able to unite and develop the same state capacity. Andreas Wimmer (2018) juxtaposes the experiences of Botswana and Somalia arguing that prior state capacity in Botswana facilitated successful nation-building since state elites could provide basic public goods across their territory – including security, infrastructure, and rule of law – and thus establish far-reaching networks of support from different ethnic groups, rather than being limited to their own ethnic clientele. Oxana Shevel (2011) suggests that elite fragmentation hinders consensus on which group of migrants should receive preferential treatment by the state, and counterintuitively creates political space for more receptive and nondiscriminatory refugee policies. Finally, Maya Tudor (2013) argues that the degree of elite cohesion in their

---

[147] Griffiths et al. 2023; Coggins 2011.

nationalist movements brokered postindependence regime stability in India as compared to Pakistan.

Taken together, these comparative works all suggest that elite fragmentation around national narratives not only exists but that its variation meaningfully explains important political outcomes ranging from tax capacity, migration policy, political stability, and public goods provision.

3.2 Popular Fragmentation

The second dimension along which national communities vary is *popular fragmentation*. Popular fragmentation refers to the degree of cohesion among the population within a territory, or members of a stateless nationalist movement, over the definition of the nation. Just as elites can be more or less united around narratives of the nation, popular understandings of the nation can also be more or less united. Everyday understandings of national narratives are typically most clearly conveyed in the form of history books, which teach stories about what characteristics define the nation. National narratives are also cued in popular imagination in more everyday forms, as Billig (1995) has established. Beyond schooling, the people are continually reminded of their relationship to the state through such qualifiers as "our" and "we" in speeches and official statements, in the omnipresent symbols of nationhood on the printed currency and on national flags, and through the celebration of national holidays through parades and festivals.[148]

Much recent scholarship has demonstrated that different popular conceptions of the nation exist and can change over time.[149] American national identity has recognized at least two distinct conceptions of national belonging, one emphasizing egalitarian/creedal aspects and another emphasizing racial/religious aspects.[150] Similarly, different ethnic groups living in Myanmar (known as Burma up until 1989) are highly fragmented as to what ethnicity and religion define the imagined community of the country.[151] Koreans are broadly united around ethnic and blood-based understandings of the national identity,[152] though this narrative has taken on new layers, including anti-colonial and anti-communist frames, around which there is more contestation today.[153] Meanwhile, the

---

[148] Billig 1995; Wedeen 2008; Skey and Antonisch 2017; Zubrzycki 2017.

[149] See the *Nationalities Papers'* special issue guest edited by Paul Goode (2020).

[150] For the classic emphasis on creedal aspects, see Smith 1997; Schildkraut 2011. For an excellent overview of regional variations, see, King, Lieberman, Ritter and Whitehouse (2009); Bonikowski and DiMaggio 2016. On Christian nationalism see Jones 2016; Whitehead and Perry 2020; Gorski et al. 2022.

[151] Callahan 2005; Lall and South 2018.   [152] Hur 2020.   [153] Jo, forthcoming.

Yugoslav national identity was relatively unified until the 1990s through homogenous portrayals of national figures, history books, and public spectacles, but popular fragmentation along ethnic/(sub-)national lines never ceased to exist.[154]

Where does popular fragmentation come from? Cohesive popular narratives of a nation often emerge in contexts with uncontested elite narratives, most typically when elites are unified through external threat or shocks or following military successes.[155] Because elites are in control of state machinery, they can use state institutions, often schools, and symbolic spaces to lower the degree of popular fragmentation.[156] But as Jo (2022) illustrates, popular narratives can also influence elite fragmentation – at least in democracies, along partisan lines. As with elite fragmentation, scholarship across different historical contexts and geographies demonstrates that variation in popular fragmentation also exists.[157] Popular fragmentation is often linked to elite fragmentation and affects a range of crucial political outcomes, as we saw in the case of Pakistan and Bangladesh.

But what are the sources of popular fragmentation? The degree of popular fragmentation has been linked to national investment in schooling, often resulting in turn from external threats. Weber's (1976) canonical study of French peasants, who identified primarily with regional identities during most of the nineteenth century, shows how peasants were turned into Frenchmen through the homogenizing reach of French schools. Darden and Mylonas (2016) show how external threats, especially those operating through the cultivation of enemies within, in areas of heightened geopolitical competition historically motivated elites to invest in the creation of shared popular narratives of the nation,[158] whereas state elites that did not face such threats did not invest in policies that foster a cohesive national narrative. Hur (2022) also traces out how elites leading the Korean nationalist movement selected symbols and narratives to create a *danil* minjok or community, descended from a singular bloodline with broad popular resonance.

In much of the world, popular fragmentation often produced through long-standing colonial practices of divide and rule, such as those pursued by the British Empire in India and Kenya, the Belgians in the Congo, the French in Syria, Lebanon, and Indochina, the Dutch in Indonesia and the Americans in the Philippines.[159] To insure against a population revolting, colonial governments

---

[154] Kong and Yeoh 1997; Liu et al. 2002.   [155] Sambanis et al. 2015.
[156] Darden and Mylonas 2016.
[157] Bonikowski and DiMaggio 2016; Chhibber and Verma 2018.
[158] See also Hintze 1975; Tilly 1990; Posen 1993; Tilly and Blockmans 1994; Herbst 2000; Mylonas 2012; Wimmer 2012.
[159] Morrock 1973: 7.

emphasized real or imagined differences within the subject population and often pitted these groups against one other. In Cyprus, for instance, the British created separate educational systems for Christian Orthodox and Muslim communities. Greece sent teachers to the schools that Greek Orthodox Cypriots attended, while Turkey sent teachers to the schools that Muslim Cypriots attended. These educational policies hardened erstwhile fluid differences between the communities and made it nigh-impossible for a common Cypriot identity to flourish. British policies fueled ethnic antagonism and ultimately took advantage of the crisis to remain present[160] and relevant postindependence. A similar story could be told of British India's partition into two (and then ultimately three) sovereign successor nation-states post 1947.

Varying levels of popular fragmentation have been shown to have important consequences for political outcomes. Darden and Grzymala-Busse (2006) show that differing patterns in the timing and content of popular national narratives introduced through state-controlled schooling explains whether Communist parties stayed in power after the collapse of the Soviet Union and the disbandment of the Warsaw Pact. Singh (2015) studies variation in a federal state and shows that in administrative units where sub-national elites successfully create a popular sub-national identity, they are more able to provide collective public goods in health and education because of the solidarity that flows from this shared identity. Popular fragmentation has long been theorized to play a pivotal role in the onset of armed conflict. Identity categories, ethnic, regional, or religious, have been proposed to have direct causal effects on the outbreak and duration of civil wars.[161] As has been well-established, when popular fragmentation assumes territorial dimensions, sub-national identities may end up generating movements seeking self-determination, leading to separatist nationalism. Within India for example, regional identities such as Kashmir and Punjab have expressly opposed accommodation with a unified India.[162] In the United States, this separatist nationalism–motivated by popular fragmentation over what it meant to be American–motivated the Civil War.

To be sure, popular and elite fragmentation typically overlap. Meadwell (1993) and Zubrzycki (2016) show that Quebec nationalism was at key stages driven by elite *and* popular support for a separate state. Thus, Canada was experiencing both elite and popular fragmentation. In the Indian case, the Nehruvian national narrative not only won out among elites (religious nationalism was deeply marginalized in the aftermath of Partition, the largest

---

[160] The Sovereign Base Areas of Akrotiri and Dhekelia are British Overseas Territories on the island of Cyprus.

[161] Goddard 2006; Cederman et al. 2013; Lieberman and Singh 2017; Kuo and Mylonas 2019.

[162] Varshney 1993.

and bloodiest migration in human history). But it also won out in terms of popular support: Hindu nationalist parties historically saw minimal electoral support (below 10 percent of the electoral vote) in the three decades after independence, with polarization around the place of Hinduism in society only rising in 1989.[163] Similarly, contestation over the inclusion of Black people in American conceptions of the nation were dominant in both popular and elite understandings of nationhood until at least the adoption of the 14th amendment to American constitution in 1868. Mavrogordatos (1983) has shown that in early twentieth-century Greece, elite and popular fragmentation over the national narrative occurred between two sides of the so-called "National Schism": the Venizelists (named after their leader, Eleftherios Venizelos) and the Anti-Venizelists. The views of the Venizelists echoed Ernest Renan's ideas as expressed in his 1882 lecture at the Sorbonne, while the view of the Anti-Venizelists was narrower and emphasized regional and ethnocultural traits.

Yet recent scholarship has also shown that elite narratives of a nation can also diverge significantly from popular narratives of a nation – in ways that are often deeply consequential for political outcomes. Hur (2022) showcases how divergence between popular and elite national narratives in Taiwan negatively affects the state's ability to call on citizens to promote public goods provision relative to Korea. Vom Hau (2009) shows that Mexican, Argentinian, and Peruvian elites all used textbooks to disseminate homogenous national narratives, but that popular embrace of these narratives varied. Relatedly, Mylonas and Shelef (2014) find that as leaders of stateless nationalist movements engage in the competition for power and survival, they alter their rhetoric about the extent of the desired homeland to meet immediate political challenges that resonate with the majority of the members of a movement. These then can become institutionalized as comprising the new territorial scope of the desired national state. Mylonas and Whalley (2022) find that states' ability to successfully gain public acceptance of pandemic-fighting measures was more difficult in contexts where the national narrative was popularly fragmented. Where instead popular narratives of nation were unified, nationalism played an important role in legitimating restrictive measures and motivating millions of people to comply with them. Taken together, such recent work highlights the importance of conceptualizing popular and elite nationalism as separate dimensions of nationalism, dimensions that can critically shape political outcomes such as voting behavior, military service, political violence, public goods provision, and secessionist war.

---

[163] Before 1980, Hindu nationalist political parties had never received ten percent of the vote in elections. Chhibber and Verma 2018.

4 How Do National Narratives Vary?

Assuming there is a sufficient cohesion among elite and popular conceptions of a nation to instantiate a single national community, its national narrative will vary along–at least–two dimensions: "ascriptiveness" and "thickness." Most nationalisms in the world, especially beyond Europe and the Americas, emerged when Indigenous elites adopted nationalism as a means of countering colonial ideologies and legitimating their efforts for independence. Yet Indigenous elites varied importantly in the types of markers that they used to construct the national narratives emerging around the globe. While some leaders utilized existing racial, religious, or ethnic cleavages to imagine their national communities, other leaders attempted to create ideals or principles that signified why a set of peoples were a nation. For example, while Pakistani and Malaysian leaders built their national narratives around the contextually fixed identities of religion and religion/ethnicity, respectively, leaders in neighboring India and Indonesia created national narratives that were not intrinsically fused with ascriptive markers but rather based upon principles: unity in diversity and *Pancasila,* respectively.

Moreover, even in cases where governing elites used relatively more ascriptive markers to build their national narratives, there was variation in how many layers were involved, how thickly imagined those narratives were. Both Pakistan and Bangladesh were states carved out of the British empire based on religious grounds, of Islam. But at their births in 1947 and 1971, respectively, Pakistani nationalism was "thinner" than Bangladesh's. We further unpack these two dimensions along which national narratives vary below.

4.1 Ascriptiveness in National Narratives

Ascriptiveness refers to the degree in which narratives of nationhood emphasize fixed, or ascriptive, forms of social identity such as race, religion, or ethnicity – identities that are socially assigned and passed through birth (hereditary) rather than chosen. Highly ascriptive national narratives are often categorized as *ethnic*, while national narratives that instead emphasize principles or ideals that are formally open to all citizens irrespective of any ascriptive identity are often categorized as *civic*.[164] While some readers may understand ascriptiveness as meaning "natural," we are using ascriptiveness in the sociological sense to denote an identity that is socially assigned but passed through birth (hereditary) rather than chosen.[165]

---

[164] Hans Kohn (1944, 1955, 1962) originally developed this distinction.   [165] Linton 1936.

We have chosen to focus on the degree of "ascriptiveness" rather than adopt the more common "civic" and "ethnic" categorization to make three conceptual moves. First, we eschew classically dichotomous discussions of "ethnic" and "civic" nationalism and instead recognize ascriptiveness as a continuous variable which invites empirical assessments. Much classic scholarship posited that ethnic versus civic understandings of nationhood were clear, dichotomous types of nationalism.[166] Yet scholars today largely agree that distinctions between ethnic and civic nationalism were often normatively rather than empirically designated. For example, most early work on American nationalism asserted that the United States had a civic national narrative until Rogers Smith's groundbreaking work evidenced that multiple, competing traditions existed,[167] including "liberalism, republicanism, and ascriptive forms of Americanism," a finding that scholars of American nationalism continue to substantiate.[168] Recent empirical work has shown that civic forms of nationalism often smuggle in ethnic characteristics.[169]

Moreover, much public commentary and some scholarly research has often defined nationalism through references to ethnicity, which would render the term ethnic nationalism redundant. For example, Gellner wrote that nationalism could even be defined as "a theory of political legitimacy, which requires that ethnic boundaries should not cut across political ones..." (Gellner 1983, 1). This association is not just a legacy of World War II, when the rise of a regime celebrating Germany's ethnically or racially defined national identity reverberated around the globe. The association between nationalism and ethnicity was further strengthened by the fact that the 1990s Yugoslav conflicts as well as post-Communist regimes' trajectories were often explained in terms of ethnic understandings of nations.[170] Our goal, however, is to conceptually delink nationalism from ethnicity.

Second, we underscore that not all ascriptive categories involve ethnic markers and that the usage of "ethnic" to denote what is in fact a broad range of socially designated identities can create discursive confusion. While some sociological and political science scholarship can understand ethnicity to encompass other identity categories such as caste and religion, everyday usage uses the term to refer exclusively to ethnic categories. Following Gerring's (1999) exhortation to use concepts that are both broadly resonant and parsimonious, we employ ascriptiveness because it adheres better to the desiderata of sound concepts.

---

[166] Zimmer 2003.   [167] Smith 1997: 550.

[168] Theiss-Morse 2009; Schildkraut 2011; Wright et al. 2012; LePore 2018; Bui 2022. See also Tamir 2020b.

[169] Nielsen 1996; Xenos 1996; Brubaker 1999; Tamir 2019; Simonsen and Bonikowski 2020.

[170] Chirot 1991; Sekulić et al. 1994.

The third reason we choose to focus on the continuum of ascriptiveness rather than engage the "civic versus ethnic" binary is that the very same building block categories of nationhood can be ascriptive or not, depending on the broad spatial and temporal context. As Zubrzycki (2001: 231) argues, "the mobilizing potential of the civic and ethnic models is constrained by specific cultural and historical legacies that frame the discursive field of the nation, as well as by specific political and institutional arrangements." Even the most classic "ascriptive" categories such as race are beginning to be less ascriptive, at least in some contexts, through widespread processes of demographic change. Notably, religion is particularly difficult to place firmly in either ascriptive or chosen categories. While one's religious affiliation can be relatively freely chosen in the United States today, one's hereditary religious category is relatively ascriptive in the context of Narendra Modi's India. Whether a particular social category is thought of as relatively fixed or relatively chosen must therefore be empirically established in a contextually specific manner.

Ascriptiveness in national narratives can also vary over time. In fact, the visibility and stickiness of ascriptive characteristics of national constitutive stories is also variable and endogenous to politics.[171] For example, the US Census counted only three ethno-racial categories in 1860, but hundreds in 2000. Today, the US Census allows respondents to (self) identify with multiple categories.

In short, the ascriptiveness of national narratives is better understood as falling along a spectrum. Dominant national narratives often lean toward a more or less ascriptive direction, thus underscoring the usefulness of ascriptiveness as one dimension of national narratives. India's founding national narrative did not embrace a particular ascriptive identity in defining the nation. Increasingly however, the majority religion of Hinduism is coming to define the national narrative.[172] The perception of ascriptiveness can vary across different age cohorts or across regions. For example, when individuals are asked in surveys how important civic and ethnic attributes are to defining a nation, cross-national results rarely cluster neatly into dichotomous categories. In the United States, Bonikowski and DiMaggio show that individuals understand American-ness to have different meanings over time, meaning that there are clear differences between groups that identify with "civic" and "ethnic" definitions of America.[173]

---

[171] Horowitz 1895; Brand 2014.   [172] Tudor 2018; Chatterji et al. 2019.
[173] Bonikowski and DiMaggio 2016.

One way to ascertain the ascriptiveness of a national narrative is to understand its national hero. Is the national hero a member of the traditional elite or "ordinary people."?[174] Just as Max Weber theorized that political order is underpinned by three ideal-type sources of legitimacy, nations can be embodied in two ideal-types of heroes. One form involves a traditional elite who serves as a focal point for the national narrative, linking past, present and future. Sometimes, as in Malaysia, the nation was embodied by sultans. Sometimes, as in Thailand and the United Kingdom, it was a monarch. Traditional elites were more likely to embody the nation when there was little sustained mass popular mobilization during the lead up to national independence – because in the face of little appetite or time to create a grassroots-based nationalist movement, Indigenous elites often built up traditional elites as embodying the nation to mobilize followers, particularly in the context of anti-colonial nationalist movements.

When the nation is embodied in a traditional ascriptive elite, then nationalism is definitionally more ascriptive because that figurehead becomes a centralized, usable symbolic resource, but one that often builds in a type of social conservatism. In Japan for example, the modern nation was defined through the emperor during the Meiji restoration of the nineteenth century. The emperor was the divine embodiment of the nation, such that the nation and the emperor were often considered synonymous. The identity between emperor and nation was used to both create the modern nation as well as change it, since changes in Japan's national narrative often entailed changes in the roles, symbols, and functions of the emperor. At the close of the nineteenth century, for example, when the Meiji elite – conservative and progressive alike – wanted to adopt and adapt western ideas of nationhood to Japan, the emperor both incarnated and motivated such changes. "The emperor was presented as the embodiment of the progressive doctrines of Meiji, the symbol not only of Japan but of Japan's capacity to propel itself energetically into the forefront of the civilized world." As Gluck describes it, "In the process of definition and diffusion, *kokutai,* the unbroken imperial tradition, was increasingly invoked as the symbolic embodiment of the nation, and the emperor acquired ever more elaborated roles as the Confucian fount of moral virtue and Shinto manifestation of a divine ancestral line." [175]

Instead of being defined through a monarch, national narratives can instead glorify 'everyday people. France is an example of a country whose founding national narrative developed during mass participation in the establishment of the modern French nation, one which rejected the monarch and aristocracy as the

---

[174] Bermeo 2020. See also Tudor and Slater 2021.   [175] Gluck 1977: 93.

symbolic basis of legitimate authority. France's national hero was a progress-oriented peasant who strove to defend the territorial integrity of the country, who would achieve upward mobility through the dint of hard work.[176] It is indeed this image of the French citizen that is celebrated in the lyrics of "*La Marseillaise,*" depicted in Delacroix's Lady Liberty painting and in French textbooks.

If a national hero is a member of a traditional, ascriptively defined elite, then *ceteris paribus,* the national narrative is more ascriptive. Yet just because the national hero is an everyday individual however, does not necessarily make the nationalism unascriptive. The Korean founding narrative, for instance, largely revolves around memories of anticolonial/anti-communist struggle *by the people*, but it is nonetheless highly ascriptive or closed about who ethnically, racially, linguistically, is "Korean."

Schools have historically played a particularly important role in popularizing the figures who represented the nation. In the closing decades of the nineteenth century, when the French began to enrol in public schooling *en masse*, schools played a pivotal role in transforming peasants into French through distributing pamphlets which little Gregoires and Pierres represented the average French person.[177] This glorification of the "average French person" was not uncontested among elites. In fact, elite fragmentation manifested itself in their choices of heroes. French republicans promoted "Marianne" as the symbol that represents opposition to monarchy, but French monarchists traditionally preferred to promote Joan of Arc, who was also not a member of the elite, but nonetheless Catholic.

Religion can also play a critical role in defining an national constitutive story. Some nation-states like Iran are based on a hybrid legitimating principle which is partly based upon national self-determination and partly based upon theocratic principles, namely the special role of Shia Islam in post-1979 Iran. Other nation-states, like France, stipulate a formal separation of Church and State, but in practice favor a particular religion's cultural practices which for example allow the wearing of small Christian symbols like the cross but not Muslim headscarves in public schools. Yet even within the context of a broadly shared religion, other social cleavages such as language and race can become so fundamentally important as to threaten a country's territorial integrity, as it did in Pakistan with the creation of Bangladesh in 1971. More generally, the ascriptiveness of religious identity is quite contextual. Judaism and Hinduism are less open to conversions from outsiders than Christianity

---

[176] Weber 1976.   [177] Weber 1976.

and Islam, which have traditionally welcomed and sometimes required outsider conversions.

Political science scholars have established that the ascriptiveness of national narratives matters for a range of outcomes, from social conservatism to genocide and regime type. Case studies of countries such as Thailand, Malaysia, and Britain show that national narratives featuring a monarch as epitomizing the nation have historically served to strengthen conservative political forces within a polity.[178] More comparatively, Straus (2015) argues that a critical variable in determining whether a national elite will perpetrate a genocide is whether a national narrative is historically ascriptive – whether the nation is centrally defined through a particular ethnic group. Straus' work empirically evaluates whether and to what degree national narratives embrace classic ethnic identities in five sub-Saharan African countries. He argues that the historical ascriptiveness of national narratives materially magnifies the possibilities of genocide. Cederman et al. (2010) argue that clear patterns of ethnic exclusion in the definition of the nation are linked to the onset of ethnic violence. And Tudor and Slater (2021) argue that the more ascriptive a national narrative, the less likely its regime is to be democratic.

In sum, the classic distinction between ethnic and civic nationalism has been shown to be considerably more complex than initially described by an earlier generation of nationalism scholars.[179] This, as well as calls for conceptual clarity, motivates our choice to propose ascriptiveness as an important dimension of nationalism. And scholarship has empirically and comparatively shown that the degree of ascriptiveness of a national narrative is consequential for outcomes such as violence and genocide.

4.2 Thickness in National Narratives

A fourth dimension along which national narratives vary is by their thickness, or by how content-laden the national narrative is. This is most clearly recognized by the number of shared national markers and the depth of those markers. Nations are often most clearly defined by who they exclude, for example, Pakistanis are not Indians, Singaporeans are not Malaysians, Canadians are not Americans, Koreans are not Japanese. For most of the world's population, nations were created in response to colonialism and were thus defined in ways to draw clear distinctions between the Indigenous population and the colonizers. But beyond this thin marker of who is *not* included, nations vary

---

[178] Hewison 1997; Smith 2006; Winichakul 2008; Fong 2009; Nairn 2011.

[179] Shulman 2002; Marx 2005; Reeskens and Wright 2010; Shevel 2010; Koopmans and Michalowski 2016; Tamir 2019b.

in *how many markers* define the nation and the *depth of articulation* for those markers, especially since nationalism is "a flexible discourse that can be wedded to a variety of political behaviors."[180] Nationalism can group together a wide variety of characteristics, including geography, language, ideology, ethnicity, race, and religion. The more a country possesses a shared history of a nation, including shared cultural markers, the thicker its national narrative.

The thickness of a national narrative is not created *deus ex machina,* but is often consciously cultivated by elites for instrumental and contextually specific purposes. Elites tend to invest in more thickly articulated national narratives when they have clear strategic reasons for doing so. A nation may well be an imagined community, but the markers of that imagining may be more expansively articulated and thus thicker in one case than in another. The nature of a national community is not just defined by the boundaries differentiating the community from outsiders, but also by the internal relationship between the members of the community and specifically, *how many* markers bind them together (language, customs, principles as well as ethnicity, religion) and how *deeply articulated* each of these markers are.

The thickness of a country's national narrative has been shown to be consequential in a variety of works. Adam Lenton (2023) traces how differing patterns of imperial expansion shaped variation in the thickness of contemporary narratives in Russia's regions. Miguel (2004) argues that state capacity in Tanzania was greater because the national independence leader made perhaps the greatest effort of any leader in sub-Saharan Africa to develop a thick Tanzanian national narrative, and propagated it through the state schooling curricula. Tudor (2013) argues that the greater thickness of India's national narrative when compared to Pakistan's, at their founding – measured through the substantive policy content discussed during the nationalist movement meetings in the years before gaining independence – critically helped postindependence regime stability in India. This thickness of the national narrative in India helped to both articulate and to instantiate a set of policy ideas, from land reform to language policy, that provided a ready blueprint of policies for elites to adapt, whereas these same policy domains led to deepening fissures in Pakistan's polity, eventually culminating in military intervention.

Recent contributions have demonstrated that it is not just elites who create thickness, but also everyday people by investing quotidian social practices with national meaning. For example, Wedeen (2008) shows how oral traditions, created and reproduced a sense of national belonging in the near absence of a state in

---

[180] Kocher et al. 2018: 150.

Yemen. Zubrzycki (2016) uses visual interpretations of a Quebecois festival to demonstrate the changing, but thick content of Quebec nationalism.

Ascriptive national narratives may more readily become 'thick' because they can absorb the readily available cultural repertoire linked to purportedly historically immutable identities. Yet ascriptiveness and thickness remain useful as analytically distinct dimensions along which national narratives may vary because a narrative can also be thickened with many markers that are not ascriptive. For instance, the Soviet Union's constitutive story had high symbolic thickness (with many symbols, figures, and principles defining the nation) but little ascriptiveness. Postindependence Pakistan by contrast has a national narrative characterized by low thickness (it was only a loose instrumentalization of Islam that brought the country into being, with no shared language, ethnicity, or principles representing the nation) but a high level of ascriptiveness since religion is an ascriptive identity in the context of South Asia.

5 When Do National Narratives Matter?

A fifth and final dimension, one that typically is measured at the level of individual attitudes, is the *salience* of a national identity relative to a multitude of other available social or political identities.[181] Scholarship has long argued that the salience of a national identity relative to other identities rises during moments of crisis (typically war, mass political violence or economic upheaval). For example, Belgian national identity, long-characterized as fragmented across elites and popular sectors, saw an appreciable rise in salience relative to other political identities following the terrorist attacks of March 2016.[182] Similar trends, in terms of the American national identity, were observed following the 9/11 attacks in the USA. More generally, crises, because they increase uncertainty and fear, have long been theorized to produce a "rally around the flag" effect.[183]

The rising salience of a national identity is not induced only by external threats but also by broader political and sports events. In postcolonial countries which witnessed mass mobilization, national identification was often high relative to other political identities following independence, which often meant that nationalist movements enjoyed a prolonged period of popularity.

---

[181] The term salience is sometimes used to signal intensity while other times it is used to indicate that an identity is ranked higher than other identities.

[182] Kuehnhanss et al. 2021.

[183] Hetherington and Nelson 2003; Esaiasson et al. 2021; Bol et al. 2021. Although there is research positing other mechanisms for this effect, such as shifts in media coverage (i.e., Berinsky 2009; Brody and Shapiro 1991).

More recently, experimental political science research has shown that national flag-burning, especially by a member of the competition group, during football matches increases the salience of in-group favoritism.[184]

Across sub-Saharan Africa, when a core ethnic group is in power, members of this group identify more with the country-level national identity, but when this group is out of power, the salience of ethnic group identity increases. [185] Relatedly, the election of a noncore group's coethnic to power has also been shown to increase the salience of belonging to the national rather than the noncore ethnic identity.[186]

Another strand of scholarship has shown that different demographic groups have distinctly different levels of national identity salience. In the United States, scholarship has revealed distinct and durable variations in American national identification across different groups, finding that one demographically distinct group has low levels of attachment to any form of national identity while another demographically distinct group is more likely to embrace all forms of national attachment.[187] In sub-Saharan Africa, a range of demographic factors – living in urban areas, having more education, and being formally employed – are all positively correlated with an increased salience of ones national identity. [188]

Recent scholarship has sought to understand the relationship between economic marginalization and the rising salience of national identities. Tamir (2019a) argues that the contemporary rise of nationalism's salience represents the reaction of unskilled labor to the growing economic gap between skilled and unskilled labor in the context of hyperglobalization. Specifically, nationalist leaders gain popularity because they propose to protect ordinary citizens from both the vicissitudes of globalization and the out-of-touch elites that promote it.[189] Miller-Idriss (2018) investigates the relationship between economic marginalization and support for nationalist movements in Europe, showing that these nationalist movements combine elements of anti-elite (populist) and anti-globalization attitudes. Colantone and Stanig (2018) show that stronger import trade shocks lead to an increase in support for nationalist and isolationist parties in Western Europe. These works agree that the migration- and generational-driven demographic changes are heightening the salience of national identities and rendering them usable for popular mobilization.

Social psychology research has made important contributions toward understanding the salience of national identity, drawing a distinction between a love of one's own country,[190] associated with healthy in-group identification,[191] and discrimination against out-group members.

---

[184] Marinthe et al. 2020.   [185] Green 2020.   [186] Koter 2019.
[187] Bonikowski and DiMaggio 2016.   [188] Robinson 2014.   [189] Zaslove 2008.
[190] Bar-Tal 1993; Bar-Tal and Staub 1997.   [191] Druckman 1994.

Political psychology research further suggests that national identification can be situationally primed for salience and is highly prone to change under threat.[192] For example, individual identification as a Hong Kong resident for a long time peacefully coexisted with identification as a Chinese national. However, economic and political changes associated with the new Hong Kong government (particularly its increasing alignment with Beijing) have turned the Hong Kong government from a source of loyalty to a source of threat. Especially among the young, the stronger one's historic identification as a Hong Kong identity, the greater the current mistrust of the Hong Kong government.[193] In sum, the time and space-variant salience of an individual's national identity is an empirically well-grounded phenomenon and has been shown to correlate with outcomes such as social trust, violence, and a range of social attitudes.

Research has not just evidenced time- and space-variant patterns of nationalism's salience, but that this salience matters for such outcomes as trust, social engagement, political mobilization, and violence. Exposure to government propaganda emphasizing the national identity in Rwanda has been shown to decrease not just the salience of ethnicity, but also to increase interethnic trust, and strengthens willingness to interact face-to-face with non-coethnics in Rwanda.[194] National football teams' victories not only make national identification more likely relative to other identities, but such victories also boost trust in other ethnicities and reduce intrastate violence.[195]

A more systematic scholarly discussion of nationalism, one which engages with five key dimensions – elite fragmentation, popular fragmentation, ascriptiveness, salience, and thickness – can strengthen the integrative and cumulative potential of nationalism studies. It is not an accident that key insights from studies of comparative democratization – for example, that the causes of democratization are different from the causes of democratic endurance and that the relative explanatory power of economic variables has declined in more recent episodes of democratization – have only been possible because scholars have agreed to conceptualize and measure the concept of democracy in similar ways.

6 Nationalism across Social Science Disciplines

Nationalism did not become a mainstream topic in political science until 1983, [196] when three influential studies of nationalism stimulated a new scholarly conversation: Benedict Anderson's (1983) *Imagined Communities*, Ernest Gellner's [2006] *Nations and Nationalism*, and Eric Hobsbawm and Terence Ranger's

---

[192] Li and Brewer 2004.   [193] Chan et al. 2020.   [194] Blouin and Mukand 2019.
[195] Depetris-Chauvin et al. 2020.
[196] Important exceptions include Arendt 1945; Coleman 1954; Emerson 1960; Rotberg 1962; Shoup 1962; Rosenblatt 1964; Rokkan 1971; Connor 1972; Young 1976.

(1983) *The Invention of Tradition*. The rich and interdisciplinary conversations which grew out of these works, as well as important world-historical events that followed on during the next decade (the fall of the Berlin Wall, the disintegration of Yugoslavia, and the Rwandan genocide) sparked renewed interest in the study of nationalism in political science.

Yet just as political science was witnessing new interest in the study of nationalism, relevant debates were growing out of other disciplines that political science has yet to fully integrate. While political science and sociological studies of nationalism have seen a good deal of cross-fertilization, research findings from other social sciences have too rarely found their way across disciplinary silos. In this section, we attempt to relate research frontiers that underscore the need for greater cross-disciplinary research.

Philosophy has long debated the merits of nationalism through normative lenses, debating human nature and political rights through the lenses of concepts such as freedom, autonomy, identity, tolerance, and self-respect. John Locke, Thomas Hobbes, and Jean-Jacques Rousseau made moral claims in favor of territorial sovereignty and an accompanying political solidarity but articulated few coherent claims regarding national solidarity.[197] Philosophers in the nineteenth century thought that the advancement of individual liberty would inevitably accompany movements toward national sovereignty. For example, John Stuart Mill wrote that: "Free institutions are next to impossible in a country made up of different nationalities. Among a people without fellow-feeling, especially if they read and speak different languages, the united public opinion, necessary to the working of representative government, cannot exist." Yet by the middle of the twentieth century, philosophers struggled to reconcile the sanguine views of national solidarity advanced by Mill and Cardinal Mazzini with its catastrophic intertwining with fascism, Nazism, Antisemitism, and racism. Perhaps unsurprisingly, the most celebrated twentieth-century philosophers – Hannah Arendt, Martha Nussbaum, John Rawls, and Charles Taylor – each recognized the importance of nationalism without making it a central object of inquiry.

Contemporary philosophical scholarship on nationalism can be conceptually divided into descriptive writing (which mirrors early political science research) and normative writing. The descriptive approach asks, "What is a nation? What is the nature of belonging to a nation?" while the normative approach asks, "Does national membership have moral worth? How much should one value national belonging relative to other identities?" We focus herein on three

---

[197] Abizadeh (2012) stresses the empirically problematic overreliance of traditional political theory on *prepolitical* grounds of legitimacy (i.e. assumed that groups predate the establishment of the basic social contract) urging scholars to "recognize that the demos is in principle unbounded" in order for democratic theory to fully avoid this "collapse of demos into nation into ethnos."

debates in normative philosophy that are critical for the empirical study of nationalism.[198]

One philosophical debate has mirrored political science's discussions over the difference, if any, between patriotism and nationalism that we discussed above. Philosophers such as Jürgen Habermas have drawn a firm conceptual line between two kinds of nationalism: one based upon real or imagined ethnic ties and another based upon a set of ideas and institutions while arguing that only the latter is morally worthy.[199] This Kantian-inspired view of the nation is in tension with a Burkean, organicist conception of a people, which sees society as an indivisible whole, united through time as well as across a particular generation. Some philosophers of this latter view theorize that a shared national identity instead promotes the legitimacy of political institutions and political stability; conduces trust and the ability to compromise among fellow citizens; and brings about social solidarity, which, in turn, leads to support for redistributive policies that undergird a successful society.[200] The debates have been almost wholly cast in normative terms however, with little recourse to empirical positivism. Cross-disciplinary work that tests the empirical assumptions of political philosophy's normative claims against empirical evidence could advance this discussion.

A second debate in normative philosophical theory which underlays much nationalism scholarship concerns the tension between liberalism and nationalism. Liberalism's growing acceptance during the 1970s was seen in the prominence of philosophers such as Robert Nozick and John Rawls, who emphasized individuals as the ultimate carriers of rights. This assumption was subsequently critiqued by communitarian philosophers for not taking seriously enough the ways in which groups were constitutive of individual identity.[201] Will Kymlicka was early to identify a conflict between the tenets of liberalism and a homogenizing nationalism. Individuals don't make choices within a vacuum, Kymlicka argued, because they are situated within a culture. It is in substantial part through a "rich and secure *cultural structure* that people can become aware, in a vivid way, of the options available to them, and intelligently examine their value."[202]

Questions of group recognition by a state were central to these philosophical debates. While many liberal philosophers assumed that the state could simply treat ethnic and cultural identities as a private matter, others

---

[198] Viroli 1995.   [199] Habermas 1996; Markell 2000.
[200] Tamir 1993; Miller 1995, 2000; Canovan 1996; Mason 1999.
[201] Nozick 1974; Sandel 1998; Rawls 1999; Walzer 1977.
[202] Kymlicka 1991: 165–166; Kymlicka 1995: 83.

such as Will Kymlicka and Yael Tamir argued that it was a "pipe-dream" to think that the state could be neutral in ways that liberal philosophers envisioned. Some identities, such as religious identities, might be left to the private sphere, but others, such as linguistic identities, were directly and deeply affected by decisions states had to make. "[T]he state cannot help but give at least partial establishment to a culture when it decides which language is to be used in public schooling, or in the provision of state services."[203]

Tamir spun out the implications for minorities: "In a world of nation-states, being a minority not only entails subjection to foreign rule, but also forfeiting recognition as a distinct national group. The most palpable expression of disregard for stateless national groups was, and still is, that international institutions such as the League of Nations or the United Nations, in spite of their names, accept only states as members."[204] Thus, state-sponsored efforts to shape states into a homeland populated by a homogeneous people, a process we described as nation-building above, invariably conflicted with minorities' demands for cultural recognition or autonomy.[205] Tamir argues that a nationalism which respects the tenets of liberalism is possible and requires acknowledging cultural differences whilst grappling, however imperfectly, with minority grievances through policy.

The "liberal individualist" vs. "communitarian group-rights" debate appears to be less pronounced today,[206] as philosophers recognise that individual and group rights are difficult to fully disentangle. Even "communitarian" defenders of nationalism and group rights sometimes claim that the reasons we must care about group rights are derived from the reasons we have to care about individuals and their rights. Michael Walzer, for instance, has argued that states' rights are derived from individuals' rights and that one important reason we have to care about states' rights is that the state is basically the only vehicle through which individuals' rights can be reliably protected.[207] Similarly, a lot of "liberal individualists" have tried to accommodate the view that belonging to/participating in certain kinds of groups is one important interest that individuals have, which should be protected, and which may ground individual rights to ensure its protection.[208]

A third relevant philosophical debate investigates nationalism's compatibility with cosmopolitanism – or the view that "one's primary moral obligations are directed to all human beings (regardless of geographical or cultural distance), and political arrangements should faithfully reflect this universal moral

---

[203] Kymlicka 1995: 111.   [204] Tamir 1993, final chapter.
[205] Han and Mylonas 2014; Mylonas 2017, 2021; Wimmer 2018.
[206] We would like to thank Lucia Rafanelli for pointing this out.   [207] Walzer 1977, 2011.
[208] For more on this, see Anna Stilz's work (2009, 2015, 2016).

obligation (in the form of suprastatist arrangements that take precedence over nation-states)."[209] The core of this debate is whether the particularism of nationalism and the universalism of cosmopolitanism are compatible. Can a cosmopolitan also be nationalist? Or, in the now infamous words of former British Prime Minister Theresa May, are citizens of the world actually citizens of nowhere, people who do not understand what the word "citizenship" means?

Philosophers agree that the nature of current political problems underscore the urgency of this debate whilst disagreeing on how to proceed. There are many varieties of cosmopolitan arguments. Some explicitly endorse world states or world democratic-decision-making procedures.[210] Yet the strong global governance structures, which they recommend to instantiate such cosmopolitan commitments, are not only lacking but appear to be in decline. Others, however, do not endorse these kinds of institutions, or their understandings of cosmopolitanism don't revolve around them. For example, Valdez (2019) argues that transnational networks of activists engaging in political struggle against imperialism and racism are the most promising form of cosmopolitanism, not suprastatist arrangements. Getachew (2019) puts forth "postcolonial cosmopolitanism," centering around a need to eliminate all forms of domination (international and domestic) from the world order, as a path that will also be liberating and bring about equality for formerly colonized peoples.[211] Rafanelli (2021) develops a type of cosmopolitanism that is not primarily about establishing supra-state institutions – though she engages with them in her theorizing – but mostly about a political struggle to achieve justice as something that is humanity's collective project.

Peter Singer argues that global problems are so intertwined that they cannot be addressed through nation-states which claim the primary loyalty of their citizens. "We need to ask whether it will, in the long run, be better if we continue to live in the imagined communities we know as nation-states, or if we begin to consider ourselves as members of an imagined community of the world. . . . Our problems are now too intertwined to be well resolved in a system consisting of nation-states, in which citizens give their primary, and near-exclusive, loyalty to their own nation-state rather than to the larger global community."[212] Singer and others unpack the structural tension between cosmopolitanism and nationalism that the rise in global economic inequality, climate change, and mass migration crises have underscored.[213]

Other philosophers argue for some compatibility between national and cosmopolitan commitments, suggesting either that nationalism is permissible

---

[209] Miscevic 2018. [210] Valentini 2013, 2014.
[211] For a critical engagement with this argument, see Rafanelli 2020. [212] Singer 2004: 171.
[213] Singer 2004; Krastev 2017.

to some forms of cosmopolitanism or even that cosmopolitanism needs to be grounded in national loyalties.[214] Kwame Anthony Appiah, for example, argues that cosmopolitanism and nationalism are fundamentally intertwined, suggesting that there is no structural tension between these two. Appiah reasons that many already simultaneously accept the tenets of cosmopolitanism's emphasis on the equal worth of humans and embrace our own individual commitments to particular communities. A tempting line of thought is that if everyone matters, then they must matter equally, and it must follow that each of us has the same moral obligations to everyone. What this reasoning misses, argues Appiah, is that "the fact of everybody's mattering equally from the perspective of universal morality does *not* mean that each one of us has the same obligations to everyone. . . . [I]t would be morally wrong *not* to favor my relatives when it comes to distributing my limited attention and time."[215]

Here too, such debates could link more closely to empirical scholarship specifically within political psychology that excavates understandings of how, why, and when humans prioritize certain social groups. For while a global community of human citizens may be a laudable goal, social psychology scholarship has recurrently and robustly demonstrated that an us-versus-them categorization is a fundamental aspect of human psychology.

Historians also debate these issues. Yuval Harari argues that human society evolved beyond small face-to-face groups only following a "cognitive revolution." Believing in shared myths or "imagined orders" was crucial to cooperation between strangers. Today, "the very survival of rivers, trees and lions depends on the grace of imagined entities such as the United States and Google."[216] While historians are generally more attuned than political scientists to the role of contingency, much historical research into nationalism has made generalizations about the concept from single-country studies, with very narrow time frames, and often using contradictory definitions that impede cross-country comparisons.

An insight that political scientists can borrow from historians is avoiding anachronism. Scholars studying nationalism often attribute certain actions to concepts and phenomena that were not politically salient or even understood by the actors under study. This practice leads to misunderstanding the ontology of the events under study and to teleological arguments. As Lawrence (2013:7) put it: "Hindsight can thus produce biased explanations. Knowledge of the outcome can lead one to erroneously believe that preferences for the outcome caused it to happen, even when the existence of such preferences has to be assumed."

---

[214] Tamir 1993; Miller 1995, 2000; Hurka 1997; Scheffler 2001.
[215] Appiah 2019: 25, emphasis added. See also Chin 2021.   [216] Harari 2014: 38.

Historical accounts are not immune to anachronism. This practice is omnipresent in national historiographies of the Balkan States. A case in point is the teleological manner in which the obligatory Greek-Turkish population exchange of 1923 has been narrated. From the contemporary vantage point, this population exchange is seen as inevitable and is often understood as an expected byproduct of the exclusionary Greek and/or Turkish understandings of nationhood. Yet a close reading of political leadership's views at the time suggests that the population exchange was not a natural extension of their national ideology – only a pragmatic choice given the adverse circumstances. Anachronism can lead us to "explain" certain events using concepts that emerged following these events.[217]

More methodologically careful comparative research would helpfully address the many normative biases that can shape historical scholarship. For example, early American scholarship has suggested that American national identity was primarily creedal,[218] whereas more recent scholarship recognizes that even in the United States – a nation of immigrants – more or less ascriptive national narratives coexist, challenging the neat distinctions between civic and ethnic narratives.[219] In keeping with the theme of normative biases, Andrew Valls (2010) rightly puzzles over the fact that community black nationalism made claims similar to minority nationalist claims for limited self-determination, yet liberal multiculturalists defended the latter while withholding support for black nationalism.

Political science is well-situated to test some of the empirical assumptions underpinning normative claims through comparative and empirically informed investigations of such questions. Historians could help by articulating testable hypotheses that could inform a coherent intellectual and policy-relevant discussion.[220] Richer comparative, cross-disciplinary, and cross-regional investigations informed by these debates could helpfully advance our understanding of a range of political outcomes while also informing policy debates.[221] For example, if cosmopolitan, national, sub-national, and local identities peacefully coexist for most individuals, then polling that presumes tensions between these identities could sustain – or worse create – false dichotomies.

Social psychology is another discipline with insights into nationalism. While the majority of political science scholarship on nationalism implicitly normatively favors the predominance of a state-level group identity, social psychologists emphasize our general social tendency toward "groupness." Generally speaking, contemporary social psychology builds upon an assumption that social behavior is driven not by individual characteristics, but by the contingent nature of social

---

[217] Mylonas 2015: 755. [218] Myrdal et al. 1944. [219] Smith 1997, 2015; Lepore 2018.
[220] Haas 1997, 2000. [221] Brubaker and Kim 2011; Ahram et al. 2018.

situations and group behavior.[222] Classic research into social identity theory showed that some degree of in-group bias is crucial to creating a positive identity and fostering individual self-esteem.[223]

At the same time, optimal distinctiveness theory postulates that humans need both to be connected with and differentiated from others, while the balance between groupness and distinctiveness is best served by identifying with a range of groups.[224] Though trust, positive affect, as well as empathy toward and cooperation with members of in-groups may well be seen as a form of discrimination of out-groups, it can and should be distinguished from the kinds of bias that actively encourage aggression and hate.[225] Moreover, strong group identification can lead individuals to prioritize the collective well-being of that group[226] even at the expense of individual interest.[227] This research can help us explore to what extent we can build national narratives that do not denigrate others.

Finally *evolutionary biologists* add further reason to think that narratives of national belonging should be taken seriously – because human cognitive psychology has been shaped over millennia to be finely attuned to narratives of belonging. Evolutionary biologists also contend that a Darwinian natural selection process has governed the transmission of culture for such a prolonged period of time that the group-oriented psychological makeup of human beings has been selected for over thousands of years: "Ethnographic evidence of the prerequisites for and operation of [cultural group selection (CGS)] in the simplest societies suggests that CGS has operated in our lineage for a few tens of millennia, if not longer. If so, the cooperative imperatives produced by rudimentary culturally transmitted institutions may well have shaped our innate social psychology. This is reflected by the observation that young children learn norms and act on them, but chimpanzee societies have, at best, rudimentary norms."[228]

The links between these fields – philosophy, history, social psychology, and evolutionary biology – have enormous potential to inform the frontiers of social science research on nationalism. If, as evolutionary biologists are beginning to argue, millennia's worth of human evolution instilled an innate need for groups and if, as many social psychologists argue, any group solidarity requires a boundary distinguishing in-groups from out-groups, then the possibilities of creating genuinely cosmopolitan commitments in the absence of other identities such as nationalism are weak.

---

[222] Ross and Nisbett 2011.   [223] Tajfel and Turner 1979.   [224] Brewer 1991.
[225] Brewer 1991; see also Levin and Sidanius 1999.
[226] Brewer 1991; De Cremer and Van Vugt 1999.   [227] De Cremer and van Dijk 2002.
[228] Richerson et al. 2016: 16.

7 Conclusion

Nationalism is as relevant to political science in the twenty-first century as it was in the twentieth century. The rise of so-called new nationalisms in recent decades has been met with derision among a wide array of leaders who associate nationalism with xenophobia, discrimination, and aggression. In 2018, French President Emmanuel Macron called on world leaders to reject nationalism, then-German Chancellor Angela Merkel warned that "blinkered nationalist views may gain ground once again"[229] and then-European Commission President Jean-Claude Juncker asserted that "unchecked nationalism is riddled with both poison and deceit."[230] Such denunciations recall a similarly strong sentiment toward nationalism in the wake of World War II, when Albert Einstein termed nationalism "an infantile disease" and Hannah Arendt linked nationalism to chauvinism.[231]

Yet nationalism has at least as often been a force for justice, freedom, and democracy. Early modern philosophers and historians borrowed from classical antiquity a respect for love of country and the accompanying spirit of self-sacrifice associated with *terra patria* (land of fathers in Latin) or πατρίς (one's fatherland in Greek) in an effort to provide foundations for modern political obligation.[232] Cicero stressed that "love of country" consists of "benevolent service for the fellow-citizens and the friends of the country."[233] When mass nationalism first emerged and spread across Europe in the early modern period, it broadly legitimated wresting power *from* monarchs in the name of self-rule by "the people" and claimed patriotism as an inclusionary ideology for all members of society, or at least all the people that fit the criteria of belonging to the modern concept of the *nation*. The idea that power was legitimated in the interests of a people was a critical motivator for the American and French revolutions, which directly paved the way for governments that were, at least in principle, responsible for representing "we the people" – the three words invoked at the start of many of the world's constitutions.

The nationalisms which emerged and spread from these revolutions embraced a set of principles which grounded citizenship in universalist liberal language, even while they also reproduced obvious inequalities: slavery, internal colonialism, and patriarchy.[234] That France's founding narrative – defined by *liberté, égalité, fraternité* – or America's founding narrative – defined by *life, liberty and the pursuit of happiness* – were not remotely fulfilled in practice, either at their founding or today, does not invalidate the fact that these principles have been used time and again to broaden the

---

[229] Irish 2018.   [230] Juncker 2018.   [231] Einstein quoted in Isaacson 2007: 386; Arendt 1945.
[232] Viroli 1995.   [233] Cicero, *De Inventione*, 2. 53. 53.   [234] Smith 1997.

ambit of "the people" within these countries. Because this formally egalitarian creed (again, severely constrained though it was by gender and race exclusions in practice) defined the American nation at its founding, Susan B. Anthony and Martin Luther King could invoke this creed and gain the support for expanding rights to previously marginalized groups.

Beyond Europe, as nationalism was borrowed and adapted across the globe during the nineteenth and twentieth centuries, it was often employed to promote more participatory and just political systems. In Latin America, "creole pioneers" used nationalism to declare independence from colonial governments that did not represent their interests and blocked their social mobility.[235] Across the postcolonial world more broadly, new nation-states achieved independence by invoking the political principle of nationalism and putting forth national narratives that in many cases continue to be important drivers of political outcomes.[236] Nationalism, the most important political ideology of the modern era, has without question *sometimes* contributed to the creation of more representative regimes.

The use of nationalism can no doubt promote such public goods as the creation of responsive governments or the protection of public health, but the invocation of nationalism is nonetheless also associated with xenophobia, aggression, and war. The prevailing negative connotations of nationalism, at least in the West, arise from nationalism's pivotal role in catastrophic twentieth-century World Wars. After witnessing how nationalism-fueled fascism led to one of the deadliest bouts of mass killings in modern times, many understandably arrived at the conclusion that nationalism was the "starkest political shame of the twentieth century."[237] For over half a century since, political leaders, scholars, and pundits across the western world have rejected nationalism as incompatible with both liberal ideals and the cosmopolitan premise of human equality.[238]

Twentieth-century European history exemplifies how nationalism *can* fuel discrimination, war, and even genocide. The Nazi party weaponized an ethno-linguistic German nationalism to legitimate Nazi aggression toward other nation-states and a range of minorities within Germany, resulting in the holocaust. More recently, Serbian nationalism was used to incite systematic rape and murder of Bosnian Muslims. And historians draw a direct causal link between Rwanda's racialized nationalism, which embraced colonial-era ethnic distinctions, and the 1994 genocide that witnessed ethnic Hutus murdering their Tutsi conationals. "More than any other

---

[235] Anderson 1983.   [236] Lawrence 2013; Tudor 2013; Tudor and Slater 2021.
[237] Dunn, 1979: 57; See also, Buell 1925.   [238] Nodia 1992.

development, the Rwandan genocide is a testimony to both the poisoned colonial legacy and nativist nationalist project that failed to transcend it."[239]

Yet even a cursory empirical examination reveals that, like several other identities, nationalisms *can* but *need not* broker such political horrors. Dozens of decolonization movements were inspired by the principles of national self-determination following World War II.[240] From a broader evolutionary perspective, "*homo sapiens* conquered this planet thanks above all to the unique human ability to create and spread fictions" that allowed them to cooperate effectively.[241] In the modern world of nation-states, nationalism has been invoked to spur on the spirit of cooperation with and self-sacrifice for complete strangers. For example, as part of a drive to ideologically popularize and institutionally instantiate "Britain" as a single imagined community, the left-leaning Labor party in Britain won the pivotal 1945 election on a manifesto that mentioned "socialist" and "socialism" three times but the words "nation" and "national" almost fifty times.[242] In the aftermath of this election, British nationalism powered a wide range of political projects, most notably the creation of its much-loved National Health Service.[243]

So while nationalisms can go – and have gone – wrong, it is clear that they don't always. Indeed, Benedict Anderson understood the power of nationalism to inspire sacrifice for the common good when he wrote

> "In an age when it is so common for progressive, cosmopolitan intellectuals to insist on the near-pathological character of nationalism, its roots in fear and hatred of the *Other*, and its affinities with racism, it is useful to remind ourselves that nations inspire love, and often profoundly self-sacrificing love. The cultural products of nationalism – poetry, prose fiction, music, plastic arts – show this love very clearly in thousands of different forms and styles. On the other hand, how truly rare it is to find *analogous* nationalist products expressing fear and loathing?"[244]

That nationalism could be used to energize various political projects was well understood by Alexis de Tocqueville (2000 [1835]: 89), who singled out nationalism and religion together as the only two forces which could unite a society: "there is in this world only patriotism, or religion, which can make all citizens walk for long towards a common goal." [245] In an age of identity politics that deconstructs and challenges large-scale communities into ever small-scale and intersectionally unique identities, particular types of nationalism have the potential to solder together diverse peoples into a common political project that

---

[239] Mamdani 2001: 38.   [240] Allman 2013.   [241] Harari 2014.   [242] Edgerton 2018.
[243] Canovan 1984.   [244] Anderson 1983: 141–142; emphasis in original.
[245] Most contemporary scholarship on nationalism finds little distinction between patriotism and nationalism. We discussed this point in Section 2.

can move beyond war-making and inspire substantial sacrifice for the common good.

As contemporary manifestations of nationalism make abundantly clear, not only is a world without nations and nationalism very far from reality,[246] but a state without a shared political identity is more likely to experience the problems faced by modern-day Somalia or Yemen, than be a peaceful political unit inhabited by undifferentiated global citizens.[247] Nationalism remains today one of the most powerful identities and ideologies around the world. At a time when the celebration of identity politics motivates the celebration of demographically ever-smaller groups, we urgently need a better understanding of what nationalism is, how it varies, and what consequences these variations have.

Despite the enduring relevance of nationalisms to contemporary politics around the globe, there is little consensus about nationalism's normative nature or its empirical dimensions in a manner that enables meaningful comparisons through time and across countries. Even within the same country at the same time, scholars have understood and operationalized nationalism in divergent ways, much like a blind man holding a different part of the proverbial elephant. Without some systematic disaggregation of the concept of nationalism, scholars can little hope to explain its comparative trends or predict its consequences.

In *Varieties of Nationalism*, we have argued for a new approach to conceptualizing nationalism that is at once historically contextual and multidimensional. Much like scholars of democracy set out their definitions of democracy by choosing among the major sub-types of democracy we argue that scholars of nationalism need to identify what part of nationalism they aim to study and explicitly situate their research questions vis-à-vis the five dimensions along which nationalisms vary: elite fragmentation and *popular fragmentation* at the administrative unit (or movement) level; *ascriptiveness* and *thickness* at the constitutive story level; and *salience* at the individual identity level. Encouraging scholars to specify *what dimension* of nationalism they propose to investigate and properly situating their cases based on their characteristics enables a more systematic discussion of the phenomenon across not only political science, but history, sociology, psychology, and philosophy.

Nations and nationalisms characterized by deep and enduring elite and popular fragmentations are unlikely to thrive and will be in recurrent danger of fragmenting into separate national communities. National communities with elite and popular cohesion are more likely to be able to solve important

---

[246] Wimmer 2019.   [247] Fukuyama 2018.

collective action problems, especially when the cohesive narratives held by elites and by individuals are aligned. National communities with high elite but low popular fragmentation, or vice versa, are more prone to deadlocked politics.

Just as with most ideologies, nationalism no doubt possesses the possibility of motivating exclusion and violence. And various configurations of national understandings, when interacting with particular political contexts, are more likely to militate toward violence – a question for future research. We hypothesize that more ascriptive understandings of nationhood are, *ceteris paribus*, more likely to discriminate against the long-term inclusion of migrants or refugees than less ascriptive ones. Similarly, moments when the salience of national identity is relatively high for a relatively high proportion of individuals, individuals are more likely to act in ways that prioritize that identity.

At each point in time, we could describe a country's *variety of nationalism* by assigning values for each one of these five dimensions. Situating nationalism around our five dimensions is a first step in identifying similarities and differences across cases. Two countries may be considered to have similar nationalisms because they both have less ascriptive (traditionally more civic) definitions of nationhood, but one may have a thicker national narrative. Acknowledging such differences is important, both in terms of appropriately comparing and thus ultimately for drawing policy conclusions.

While we propose that these five dimensions reflect a broad range of scholarly research, we do not argue that any particular dimension is more important – nor do we preclude that future research will unpack new ones. Rather, our intention in this Element is to conceptualize how major veins of scholarship on nationalism have studied it. We do claim that these five dimensions are reflected in major scholarly conceptions of nationalism; that each dimension is logically distinct; that scholars have shown that variations in these dimensions meaningfully explain important political phenomena; and that scholars who more clearly specify which dimension of nationalism they are studying can help build cumulative knowledge in the field, enabling us to see the elephant that is nationalism.

References

Abdelal, R., Herrera, Y. M., Johnston, A. I., and McDermott, R. (eds.). 2009. *Measuring Identity: A Guide for Social Scientists*. New York, NY: Cambridge University Press.

Abizadeh, A. 2012. "On the demos and its kin: Nationalism, democracy, and the boundary problem." *American Political Science Review*, 106(4), 867–882.

Ahram, A. I., Köllner, P., and Sil, R. (eds.). 2018. *Comparative Area Studies: Methodological Rationales and Cross-regional Applications*. New York, NY: Oxford University Press.

Aktürk, Ş. 2012. *Regimes of Ethnicity and Nationhood in Germany, Russia, and Turkey*. New York: Cambridge University Press.

Allman, J. 2013. "Between the present and history: African nationalism and decolonization." In Parker J. and Reid R. (eds.), *The Oxford Handbook of Modern African History*. New York: Oxford University Press, pp. 224–240.

Allport, G. W., Clark, K., and Pettigrew, T. 1954. *The Nature of Prejudice*. New York: Basic Books.

Amoretti, U. M., and Bermeo, N. G. (eds.). 2004. *Federalism and Territorial Cleavages*. Baltimore: Johns Hopkins University Press.

Anderson, B. 1983. *Imagined Communities: Reflections on the Origin and Spread of Nationalism*. London: Verso.

Arendt, H. 1945. "Imperialism, nationalism, chauvinism." *The Review of Politics*, 7(4), 441–463.

Arendt, H. 1963. *On Revolution*. New York: Viking.

Appiah, K. A. 2018. *The Lies that Bind: Rethinking Identity. Creed, Country, Colour, Class, Culture*. London: Profile Books.

Appiah, K. A. 2019. "The importance of elsewhere: In defense of cosmopolitanism." *Foreign Affairs*, 28(2), 20–26.

Baker, C. 2015. *The Yugoslav Wars of the 1990s*. Bloomsbury.

Balcells, L. 2013. "Mass schooling and Catalan nationalism." *Nationalism and Ethnic Politics*, 19(4), 467–486.

Banac, I. 1984. *The National Question in Yugoslavia: Origins, History, Politics*. Ithaca, NY: Cornell University Press.

Bar-Tal, D. 1993. "Patriotism as fundamental beliefs of group members." *Politics and the Individual*, 3(2), 45–62.

Bar-Tal, D. E. and Staub, E. E. 1997. *Patriotism: In the Lives of Individuals and Nations*. Chicago, IL: Nelson-Hall Publishers.

Barrington, L. W. 1997. "'Nation' and 'nationalism': The misuse of key concepts in political science." *PS: Political Science & Politics, 30*(4), 712–716.

Basta, K. 2021. *The Symbolic State: Minority Recognition, Majority Backlash, and Secession in Multinational Countries*. Kingston: McGill-Queen's Press

Bayram, A. B. 2019. "Nationalist cosmopolitanism: The psychology of cosmopolitanism, national identity, and going to war for the country." *Nations and Nationalism, 25*, 757–781.

Bearak, M. 2016. "Theresa May criticized the term "citizen of the world." But half the world identifies that way." *The Washington Post*. October 5. www.washingtonpost.com/news/worldviews/wp/2016/10/05/theresa-may-criticized-the-term-citizen-of-the-world-but-half-the-world-identifies-that-way/.

Beissinger, M. R. 2002. *Nationalist Mobilization and the Collapse of the Soviet State*. New York: Cambridge University Press.

Berinsky, A. J. 2009. *In Time of War*. Chicago, IL: University of Chicago Press.

Berlin, I. 1969. *Four Essays on Liberty*. Oxford, England: Oxford University Press.

Bermeo, N. G. 2020. *Ordinary People in Extraordinary Times*. Princeton, N.J: Princeton University Press.

Bhambra, G. K. 2017. "Brexit, Trump, and 'methodological whiteness': On the misrecognition of race and class." *The British Journal of Sociology, 68*, S214–S232.

Biden, Joseph R. 2022. "Remarks by President Biden on the continued battle for the soul of the nation." Philadelphia, Pennsylvania. September 1. www.whitehouse.gov/briefing-room/speeches-remarks/2022/09/01/remarks-by-president-bidenon-the-continued-battle-for-the-soul-of-the-nation/.

Bieber, F. 2022. "Global nationalism in times of the COVID-19 pandemic." *Nationalities Papers, 50*(1), 13–25.

Billig, M. 1995. *Banal Nationalism*. London: Sage

Blackwill, R. D. and Campbell, K. M. 2016. *Xi Jinping on the global stage: Chinese foreign policy under a powerful but exposed leader*. New York: Council on Foreign Relations Press.

Blank, T., and Schmidt, P. 2003. "National identity in a united Germany: Nationalism or patriotism? An empirical test with representative data." *Political Psychology, 24*(2), 289–312.

Blouin, A., and Mukand, S. W. 2019. "Erasing ethnicity? Propaganda, nation building, and identity in Rwanda." *Journal of Political Economy, 127*(3), 1008–1062.

Boix, C. 2019. *Democratic Capitalism at the Crossroads: Technological Change and the Future of Politics*. Princeton, NJ: Princeton University Press.

Bol, D., Giani, M., Blais, A., and Loewen, P. J. 2021. "The effect of COVID-19 lockdowns on political support: Some good news for democracy?" *European Journal of Political Research, 60*(2), 497–505.

Bonikowski, B. 2016. "Nationalism in settled times." *Annual Review of Sociology*, *42*, 427–449.

Bonikowski, B. and DiMaggio, P. 2016. "Varieties of American popular nationalism." *American Sociological Review*, *81*(5), 949–980.

Brand, L. A. 2014. *Official Stories: Politics and National Narratives in Egypt and Algeria*. Palo Alto, CA: Stanford University Press.

Breuilly, J. (ed.). 2013. *The Oxford Handbook of the History of Nationalism*. Oxford: Oxford University Press.

Brewer, M. B. 1991. "The social self: On being the same and different at the same time." *Personality and Social Psychology Bulletin*, *1*(5), 475–482.

Brody, R. A., and Shapiro, C. R. 1991. "The rally phenomenon in public opinion." In *Assessing the President: The Media, Elite Opinion, and Public Support*, pp. 45–78. Stanford: Stanford University Press.

Brown, K. 2017. "The powers of Xi jinping." *Asian Affairs*, *48*(1), 17–26.

Brubaker, R. 1992. *Citizenship and Nationhood in France and Germany*. Cambridge, MA: Harvard University Press.

Brubaker, R. 1996. *Nationalism Refrained: Nationhood and the National Question in the New Europe*. Cambridge: Cambridge University Press.

Brubaker, R. 1999. "The Manichean myth: Rethinking the distinction between 'civic'and 'ethnic'nationalism." In H. Kriesi K. Armington, and H. Siegrist (eds.), *Nation and National Identity: The European Experience in Perspective*. pp. 55–71. Zurich: Ruegger.

Brubaker, R. 2004. *Ethnicity without Groups*. Cambridge, MA: Harvard University Press.

Brubaker, R. 2017. "Why populism?" *Theory and Society*, *46*(5), 357–385.

Brubaker, R., and Kim, J. 2011. "Transborder membership politics in Germany and Korea." *European Journal of Sociology*, *52*(1), 21–75.

Brubaker, R., Margit, F., Jon, F., and Liana, G. 2006. *Nationalist Politics and Everyday Ethnicity in a Transylvanian Town*. Princeton, NJ: Princeton University Press

Buell, R. L. 1925. *International Relations*. New York: Henry Holt and Co.

Bui, P. 2022. Defining American National Identity: An Exploration into Measurement and Its Outcomes. *Nationalities Papers*, 1–19. doi:10.1017/nps.2021.79.

Callahan, M. P. 2005. *Making Enemies: War and State Building in Burma*. Ithaca, NY: Cornell University Press.

Canovan, M. 1984. "'People', politicians and populism." *Government and Opposition*, *19*(3), 312–327.

Canovan, M. 1996. *Nationhood and Political Theory*. Cheltenham: Edward Elgar.

Canovan, M. 2000. "Patriotism is not enough." *British Journal of Political Science, 30*(3), 413–432.

Cederman, L. E., Wimmer, A., and Min, B. 2010. "Why do ethnic groups rebel? New data and analysis." *World Politics, 62*(1), 87–119.

Cederman, L. E., Gleditsch, K. S., and Buhaug, H. 2013. *Inequality, Grievances, and Civil War.* New York: Cambridge University Press.

Chandra, K. (ed.). 2012. *Constructivist Theories of Ethnic Politics.* New York: Oxford University Press.

Chandra, K. 2006. "What is ethnic identity and does it matter?" *Annual Review of Political Science, 9,* 397–424.

Chang, M. H. 1998. "Chinese irredentist nationalism: The magician's last trick." *Comparative Strategy, 17*(1), 83–100.

Charnysh, V., Lucas, C., and Singh, P. 2014. "The ties that bind: National identity salience and pro-social behavior toward the ethnic other." *Comparative Political Studies,* 48(3), 267–300.

Charnysh, V., Lucas, C., and Singh, P. 2015. "The Ties That Bind: National Identity Salience and Pro-Social Behavior Toward the Ethnic Other." *Comparative Political Studies,* 48(3), 267–300.

Chatterji, A. P., Hansen, T.B. and Jaffrelot, C. eds., 2019. *Majoritarian state: How Hindu nationalism is changing India.* New York, NY: Oxford University Press.

Chhibber, P. K., and Verma, R. 2018. *Ideology and Identity: The Changing Party Systems of India.* New York: Oxford University Press.

Chin, C. 2021. "Multiculturalism and nationalism: Models of belonging to diverse political community." *Nations and Nationalism, 27*(1), 112–129.

Chirot, D. 1991. "What Hapened in Eastern Europe in 1989?." *Praxis International, 11*(3+ 4), 278–305.

Citrin, J., Haas, E. B., Muste, C., and Reingold, B. 1994. "Is American nationalism changing? Implications for foreign policy." *International Studies Quarterly, 38*(1), 1–31.

Coggins, B. 2011. "Friends in high places: International politics and the emergence of states from secessionism." *International Organization, 65*(3), 433–467.

Colantone, I., and Stanig, P. 2018. "The trade origins of economic nationalism: Import competition and voting behavior in Western Europe." *American Journal of Political Science, 62*(4), 936–953.

Coleman, J. S. 1954. "Nationalism in tropical Africa." *The American Political Science Review, 48*(2), 404–426.

Collier, D., and Levitsky, S. 1997. "Democracy with adjectives: Conceptual innovation in comparative research." *World Politics, 49*(3), 430–451. https://doi.org/10.1353/wp.1997.0009.

Connor, W. 1972. "Nation-building or nation-destroying?" *World Politics*, 24 (3), 319–355.

Connor, W. 1978. "A nation is a nation, is a state, is an ethnic group, is a . . .?" *Ethnic and Racial Studies*, *1*(4), 377–400.

Connor, W. 1984. *The National Question in Marxist-Leninist Theory and Strategy*. Princeton, NJ: Princeton University Press.

Connor, W. 1994. *Ethnonationalism: The Quest for Understanding*. Princeton, NJ: Princeton University Press.

Coppedge, M. 2002. "Democracy and dimensions: Comments on Munck and Verkuilen." *Comparative Political Studies*, *35*(1), 35–39.

Corcuff, S. and Edmondson, R. 2002. *Memories of the future: National identity issues and the search for a new Taiwan*. London: ME Sharpe.

Darden, K., and Grzymala-Busse, A. 2006. "The great divide: Literacy, nationalism, and the communist collapse." *World Politics*, *59*(1), 83–115.

Darden. K., and Mylonas, H. 2016. "Threats to territorial integrity, national mass schooling, and linguistic commonality." *Comparative Political Studies*, *49*(11), 1446–1479.

Dayal, H. 2021. "Jharkhand: The ascendance of the BJP as a dominant party." In S. Shastri, A. Kumar, Y. S. Sisodia (eds.), *Electoral Dynamics in the States of India*. Routledge London: Routledge India, pp. 243–254.

De Bolle, M., and Zettelmeyer, J. 2019. Measuring the rise of economic nationalism. *Peterson Institute for International Economics Working Paper*, 19–15.

De Cremer, D., and Van Vugt, M. 1999. "Social identification effects in social dilemmas: A transformation of motives." *European Journal of Social Psychology*, *29*(7), 871–893.

De Tocqueville, A. 2000(1835). *Democracy in America*, ed. and trans. H. C. Mansfield, D. Winthrop. Chicago, IL: University of Chicago Press.

Deutsch, K. 1953. *Nationalism and Social Communication: An Inquiry into the Foundations of Nationality*. Cambridge, MA: MIT Press.

Deutsch, K. 1961. "Social mobilization and political development." *American Political Science Review*, *55*(3), 493–514.

Deutsch, K. 1969. *Nationalism and Its Alternatives*. New York:Alfred A. Knopf.

Depetris-Chauvin, E., Durante, R., and Campante, F. 2020. "Building nations through shared experiences: Evidence from African Football." *American Economic Review*, *110*(5), 1572–1502.

Ding, I., and Hlavac, M. 2017. "'Right' choice: Restorative nationalism and right-wing populism in Central and Eastern Europe." *Chinese Political Science Review*, *2*(3), 427–444.

Drakulić, S. 1993. *The Balkan Express: Fragments from the Other Side of War.* New York: W. W. Norton, pp. 50–52.

Druckman, D. 1994. "Nationalism, patriotism, and group loyalty: A social psychological perspective." *Mershon International Studies Review, 38*(1), 43–68.

Dunn, J. 1979. *Western Political Theory in the Face of the Future.* New York, NY: Cambridge University Press.

Dyrstad, K. 2012. "After ethnic civil war: Ethno-nationalism in the Western Balkans." *Journal of Peace Research, 49*(6), 817–831.

Edgerton, D. 2018. *The Rise and Fall of the British Nation: A Twentieth-Century History.* London: Penguin UK.

Emerson, R. 1960. *From Empire to Nation: The Rise to Self-Assertion of Asian and African Peoples.* Cambridge, MA: Harvard University Press.

Erez, L., and Laborde, C. 2020. "Cosmopolitan patriotism as a civic ideal." *American Journal of Political Science, 64*(1), 191–203.

Esaiasson, P., Sohlberg, J., Ghersetti, M., and Johansson, B. 2021. "How the coronavirus crisis affects citizen trust in institutions and in unknown others: Evidence from 'the Swedish experiment'." *European Journal of Political Research, 60*(3), 748–760.

Farage, N. 2020. Coronavirus has shown we are all nationalists now: Does Boris Johnson realise that? *Daily Telegraph*, March 12. www.telegraph.co.uk/polit ics/2020/03/12/coronavirus-has-shown-nationalists-now-does-boris-john son-realise/.

Fearon, J. D., and Laitin, D. D. 2000. "Violence and the social construction of ethnic identity." *International Organization, 54*(4), 845–877.

Fichte, J. G. 2008. *Reden an die deutsche Nation* (Vol. 588). Hamburg: Felix Meiner Verlag.

Fong, J. 2009. "Sacred nationalism: The Thai monarchy and primordial nation construction," *Journal of Contemporary Asia, 39*(4), 673–696.

Fukuyama, F. 1989. "The end of history?" *The National Interest, 16*, 3–18.

Fukuyama, F. 2018. *Identity: The Demand for Dignity and the Politics of Resentment.* New York: Farrar, Straus and Giroux.

Fukuyama, F. 2022. *Liberalism and Its Discontents.* London: Profile Books.

Garrity, M. M. 2022. *Disorderly and Inhumane: Explaining Government-Sponsored Mass Expulsion, 1900–2020.* Ph.D. Dissertation, University of Pennsylvania.

Gat, A. 2013. *Nations: The Long History and Deep Roots of Political Ethnicity and Nationalism.* New York: Cambridge University Press

Geertz, C. 1963. *Old Societies and New States: The Quest for Modernity in Asia and Africa.* London: The Free Press of Glencoe.

Geertz, C. 1973. *The Interpretation of Cultures: Selected Essays*. New York: Basic Books.

Gellner, E. 1983. *Nations and Nationalism*. Ithaca, NY: Cornell University Press.

Gellner, E. 2006. *Nations and Nationalism*. 2nd ed. Oxford: Blackwell.

Getachew, A. 2019. *Worldmaking after Empire*. Princeton, NJ: Princeton University Press.

Gluck, C. N. 1977. *Japan's Modern Myth: Ideology in the Late Meiji Period*. New York: Columbia University.

Goddard, S. E. 2006. "Uncommon ground: Indivisible territory and the politics of legitimacy." *International Organization*, *60*(1), 35–68.

Goldstein, D. M., and Hall, K. 2017. "Postelection surrealism and nostalgic racism in the hands of Donald Trump." *HAU: Journal of Ethnographic Theory*, *7*(1), 397–406.

Goode, J. P. 2020. "Everyday nationalism in world politics: Agents, contexts, and scale." *Nationalities Papers*, *48*(6), 974–982.

Gopal, S. (ed.). 1983. *Jawaharlal Nehru: An Anthology*. New Delhi: Oxford University Press.

Gorski, P. S. 2000. "The mosaic moment: An early modernist critique of modernist theories of nationalism." *American Journal of Sociology*, *105*(5), 1428–1468.

Gorski, Philip S. 2003. *The Disciplinary Revolution: Calvinism and the Rise of the State in Early Modern Europe*. Chicago, IL: University of Chicago Press.

Gorski, P. S., Perry, S. L., and Tisby, J. 2022. *The Flag and the Cross: White Christian Nationalism and the Threat to American Democracy*. New York: Oxford University Press.

Green, E. D. 2006. "Redefining ethnicity." Paper Presented at the *47th Annual International Studies Association Convention*, San Diego.

Green, E. 2020. "Ethnicity, national identity and the state: Evidence from SSA." *British Journal of Political Science,* *50*(2), 757–779.

Greenfeld, L. 1992. *Nationalism: Five Roads to Modernity*. Cambridge, MA: Harvard University Press.

Griffiths, R. D., Pavković, A., and Radan, P. (eds.). 2023. *The Routledge Handbook of Self-Determination and Secession*. London: Taylor & Francis.

Grzymala-Busse, A. 2020. "Beyond war and contracts: The medieval and religious roots of the European state." *Annual Review of Political Science*, *23*, 19–36.

Haas, Ernst B. 1997. *Nationalism, Liberalism and Progress: The Rise and Decline of Nationalism*. Vol. 1. Ithaca, NY: Cornell University Press.

Haas, Ernst B. 2000. *Nationalism, Liberalism and Progress: The Dismal Fate of New Nations*. Vol. 2. Ithaca, NY: Cornell University Press.

Habermas, J. 1976. *Können komplexe Gesellschaften eine vernünftige Identität ausbilden? Frankfurt am Main:* Suhrkamp Verlag, pp. 92–126.

Habermas, J. 1989. *The Structural Transformation of the Public Sphere*, trans. T. Burger. Cambridge, MA: MIT Press.

Habermas, J. 1996. *Between Facts and Norms: Contribution to a Discourse Theory of Law and Democracy*. Cambridge: Polity Press.

Hale, H. E. 2004. "Explaining ethnicity." *Comparative Political Studies*, *37*(4), 458–485.

Han, E., and Mylonas, H. 2014. "Interstate relations, perceptions, and power balance: Explaining China's policies toward ethnic groups, 1949–1965." *Security Studies,23*, 148–181.

Harari, Y. N. 2014. *Sapiens: A Brief History of Humankind*. New York: Random House.

Hastings, A. 1997. *The Construction of Nationhood: Ethnicity, Religion and Nationalism*. New York: Cambridge University Press.

Hechter, M. 2013. *Alien Rule*. New York: Cambridge University Press.

Hechter, M. 2000. *Containing Nationalism*. Oxford: Oxford University Press.

Hegel, G. W. F. 1830. *Enzyklopädie der philosophischen Wissenschaften im Grundrisse*, sec. 549.

Herbst, J. 2000. *States and Power in Africa*. Princeton, NJ: Princeton University Press.

Herder, Johann Gottfried. 2004. *Another Philosophy of History and Selected Political Writings*. Translated and edited by Evrigenis, I., and Pellerin, D. Indianapolis, IN: Hackett.

Hetherington, M. J., and Nelson, M. 2003. "Anatomy of a rally effect: George W. Bush and the war on terrorism." *PS: Political Science & Politics*, *36*(1), 37–42.

Hewison, K. 1997. "The monarchy and democratisation." In K. Hewison (ed.), *Political Change in Thailand. Democracy and Participation*. London: Routledge, pp. 58–74.

Hill, F. 2022. Putin's endgame: A conversation with Fiona Hill. *The New York Times*, March 11. www.nytimes.com/2022/03/11/podcasts/the-daily/fiona-hill-ukraine-russia-ezra-klein.html.

Hill, F., and Stent, A. 2022. The world Putin wants. *Foreign Affairs*, August 25. www.foreignaffairs.com/russian-federation/world-putin-wants-fiona-hill-angela-stent.

Hinkle, S. and Brown, R. 1990. Intergroup comparisons and social identity: Some links and lacunae. In D. Abrams, and M. A. Hogg (eds.), *Social Identity Theory Constructive and Critical Advances*, pp. 48–70.

Hintze, O. 1975. "Military organization and the organization of the state." In F. Gilbert (ed.), *The Historical Essays of Otto Hintze*. New York: Oxford University Press, pp. 178–215.

Hobsbawm, E., and Ranger, T. (eds.). 1983. *The Invention of Tradition*. Cambridge: Cambridge University Press.

Horowitz, D. L. 1985. *Ethnic Groups in Conflict, Updated Edition with a New Preface*. Berkeley, CA: University of California Press.

Hur, A., 2020. "Citizen duty and the ethical power of communities: Mixed-method evidence from East Asia." *British Journal of Political Science*, 50(3), 1047–1065.

Hur, A. 2022. *Narratives of Civic Duty: How National Stories Shape Democracy in Asia*. Ithaca, NY: Cornell University Press.

Hurka, T. (1997). "The Justification of National Partiality." In McKim R. and McMahan J. (eds.), *The Morality of Nationalism*. New York, NY: Oxford University Press.

Hutchinson J. and Smith A. D. 1994. *Nationalism*. New York, NY: Oxford University Press.

Irish, J. 2018. Macron, Merkel defend multilaterism as Trump avoids peace forum. *Reuters,* November 11. www.reuters.com/article/us-peace-summit/macron-merkel-defend-multilaterism-as-trump-avoids-peace-forum-idUSKCN1NG0PB.

Isaacson, W. 2007. *Einstein: His Life and Universe*. New York: Simon & Schuster.

Janowitz, M., 1983. *The Reconstruction of Patriotism: Education for Civic Consciousness*. Chicago, IL: University of Chicago Press.

Jones, R. 2016. *The End of White Christian America*. New York: Simon & Schuster.

Jalal, A. 2014. *The Struggle for Pakistan: A Muslim Homeland and Global Politics*. Cambridge, MA: Harvard University Press.

Jenne, E., and Mylonas, H. 2023. "Ethnicity and nationalism in the study of international relations." In Cameron G. Thies (ed.), *Handbook of International Relations*. Northhampton: Edward Elgar.

Jo, E. A. 2022. Memory, Institutions, and the Domestic Politics of South Korean–Japanese Relations. *International Organization*, 76(4), 767–798.

Jo, E. A. forthcoming. *Past as Prologue: Founding Stories and Narrative Democratization in South Korea and Taiwan*. Doctoral Dissertation, Cornell University.

Juncker, J.-C. 2018. Annual state of the EU address by the president at the European Parliament. https://ec.europa.eu/info/priorities/state-union-speeches/state-union-2018_en.

Jwaideh, W. 2006. *The Kurdish National Movement: Its Origins and Development*. Syracuse, New York: Syracuse University Press.

Kamradt-Scott, A. 2020. Why 'vaccine nationalism' could doom plans for global access to a Covid-19 vaccine. *The Conversation*. September 7. https://thecon versation.com/why-vaccine-nationalism-could-doom-plan-for-global-access-to-a-covid-19-vaccine-145056.

King, D., Lieberman, R. C., Ritter, G., & Whitehead, L. (eds.). 2009. Democratization in America: A Comparative-Historical Analysis. Baltimore, MD: Johns Hopkins University Press.

Kocher, M. A., Lawrence, A. K., and Monteiro, N. P. 2018. "Nationalism, collaboration, and resistance: France under Nazi occupation." *International Security*, *43*(2), 117–150.

Kohn, H. 1944. *The Idea of Nationalism: A Study in Its Origins and Background*. New York: Macmillan.

Kohn, H. 1955. *Nationalism: Its Meaning and History*. New York: Van Nostrand.

Kohn, H. 1962. *The Age of Nationalism: The First Era of Global History*. New York: Harper and Row.

Kohn, M. L. 1987. "Cross-National Research as an Analytic Strategy: American Sociological Association, 1987 Presidential Address." *American Sociological Review*, *52*(6), 713–731.

Kong, L., and Yeoh, B. S. 1997. "The construction of national identity through the production of ritual and spectacle: An analysis of National Day parades in Singapore." *Political Geography*, *16*(3), 213–239.

Koopmans, R., and Michalowski, I. 2016. "Why do states extend rights to immigrants? Institutional settings and historical legacies across 44 countries worldwide." *Comparative Political Studies*, *50*(1), 41–47.

Kosterman, R., and Feshbach, S. 1989. "Toward a measure of patriotic and nationalistic attitudes." *Political Psychology*, *10*(2), 257–274.

Koter, D. 2019. "Presidents' ethnic identity and citizens' national attachment in Africa." *Nationalism and Ethnic Politics* 25(2), 133–151.

Kothari, R. 1964. "The congress 'system' in India." *Asian Survey*, *4*(12), 1161–1173.

Krasner, S. D. 1999. *Sovereignty: Organized Hypocrisy*. Princeton, NJ: Princeton University Press.

Krastev, I. 2017. *After Europe*. Philadelphia, PA: University of Pennsylvania Press.

Kuehnhanss, C.R., Holm, J. & Mahieu, B. 2021. Rally 'round which flag? Terrorism's effect on (intra)national identity. *Public Choice* 188: 53–74.

Kukic, L. 2019. The last Yugoslavs: Ethnic diversity, national identity, and civil war. *LSE Economic Working Papers* No. 300.

Kulyk, V. 2014. "Ukrainian nationalism since the outbreak of Euromaidan." *Ab Imperio*, *3*, 94–122.

Kuo, K., and Mylonas, H. 2019. "Nation-building and the role of identity in civil wars." *Ethnopolitics*, *21*(1), 1–21.

Kuzio, T. 2016. *Russian National Identity and the Russia-Ukraine Crisis*. Bundesakademie für Sicherheitspolitik. Security Policy Working Paper, No. 20/2016.

Kymlicka, W. 1995. *Multicultural Citizenship: A Liberal Theory of Minority Rights*. Oxford: Clarendon Press.

Kymlicka, W. 1991. *Liberalism, Community, and Culture*. New York: Oxford University Press.

Laitin, D. 1998. *Identity in Formation: The Russian-Speaking Populations in the Near Abroad*. Ithaca, NY: Cornell University Press.

Laitin, D. 2007. *Nations, States, and Violence*. New York: Oxford University Press.

Lawrence, A. 2013. *Imperial Rule and the Politics of Nationalism: Anti-colonial Protest in the French Empire*. New York: Cambridge University Press.

Levin, S., and Sidanius, J. 1999. "Social dominance and social identity in the United States and Israel: Ingroup favoritism or outgroup derogation?" *Political Psychology*, *20*(1), 99–126.

Li, Q., and Brewer, M. B. 2004. "What does it mean to be an American? Patriotism, nationalism, and American identity after 9/11." *Political Psychology*, *25*(5), 727–739.

Lieberman, E., and Singh, P. 2017. "Census enumeration and group conflict: A global analysis of the consequences of counting." *World Politics*, *69*(1), 1–53.

Lieberman, E. 2003. *Race and Regionalism in the Politics of Taxation in Brazil and South Africa*. New York: Cambridge University Press.

Linton, R. 1936. *Status and Role: The Study of Man*. New York: Appleton-Century-Crofts.

Lipset, S. M. 1963. *The First New Nation: The United States in Historical and Comparative Perspective*. New York: Basic Books.

Liu, J. H., Lawrence, B., Ward, C., and Abraham, S. 2002. "Social representations of history in Malaysia and Singapore: On the relationship between national and ethnic identity." *Asian Journal of Social Psychology*, *5*(1), 3–20.

Lee, T. 2009. "Between social theory and social science practice: Toward a new approach to the survey measurement of 'Race'." In R. Abdelal, Y. Herrera,

A. Johnston, and R. McDermott (eds.), *Measuring Identity: A Guide for Social Scientists*. Cambridge: Cambridge University Press, pp. 113–144.

Lenton, A. C. 2021. "Office politics: Tatarstan's presidency and the symbolic politics of regionalism." *Russian Politics*, *6*(3), 301–329. https://doi.org/10.30965/24518921-00603002.

Lenton, A. C. 2023. *Echoes of Empire: Subnationalism and Political Development in the Russian Federation*. PhD Dissertation, George Washington University.

Lepore, J. 2018. *These Truths: A History of the United States*. New York: W. W. Norton.

Levinger, M., and Lytle, P. F. 2001. "Myth and mobilisation: The triadic structure of nationalist rhetoric." *Nations and Nationalism*, *7*(2), 175–194.

Malešević, S. 2002. *Ideology, legitimacy and the new state: Yugoslavia, Serbia and Croatia*. London: Routledge.

Malešević, S. 2013. *Nation-States and Nationalisms: Organization, Ideology and Solidarity*. London: Polity.

Malešević, S. 2019. *Grounded Nationalisms: A Sociological Analysis*. Cambridge: Cambridge University Press.

Mamdani, M. 2001. *When Victims become Killers: Colonialism, Nativism and the Genocide in Rwanda*. Princeton, NJ: Princeton University Press.

Marinthe, G., Falomir-Pichastor, J. M., Testé, B., and Kamiejski, R. 2020. "Flags on fire: Consequences of a national symbol's desecration for intergroup relations." *Group Processes & Intergroup Relations*, *23*(5), 744–760.

Markell, P. 2000. "Making affect safe for democracy: On 'constitutional patriotism'." *Political Theory*, *28*(1), 38–63.

Marx, A. 2005. *Faith in Nation: Exclusionary Origins of Nationalism*. New York: Oxford University Press.

Marx, A. W. 1998. *Making Race and Nation: A Comparison of South Africa, the United States, and Brazil*. New York: Cambridge University Press.

Mason, A. 1999. "Political community, liberal-nationalism, and the ethics of assimilation." *Ethics*, *109*(2), 261–286.

Mavrogordatos, G. Th. 1983. *Stillborn Republic: Social Coalitions and Party Strategies in Greece, 1922–1936*. Berkeley, CA: University of California Press.

Mavrogordatos, G. Th. 2020. *Εθνική ολοκλήρωση και διχόνοια: η ελληνική περίπτωση*. [*National Integration and Discord: The Greek Case*]. Athens: Patakis.

McGrath, A. 1998. *The Destruction of Pakistan's Democracy*. Oxford: Oxford University Press (Oxford Pakistan paperbacks).

Mead, E. D. 1882. "Hegel's philosophy of the state." *The Journal of Speculative Philosophy*, *16*(2), 194–208.

Meadwell, H. 1993. "The politics of nationalism in Quebec." *World Politics, 45* (2), 203–241.

Miguel, T. 2004. "Tribe or nation? Nation building and public goods in Kenya v. Tanzania. " *World Politics, 56*(3), 327–362.

Miller, D. 1995. *On Nationality.* London: Clarendon Press.

Miller, D. 2000. *Citizenship and National Identity.* London: Polity.

Miller-Idriss, C. 2018. *The Extreme Gone Mainstream.* Princeton, NJ: Princeton University Press.

Miscevic, N. 2018. "Nationalism." *The Stanford Encyclopedia of Philosophy.* https://plato.stanford.edu/archives/sum2018/entries/nationalism/.

Morrock, R. 1973. "Heritage of strife: The effects of colonialist 'divide and rule' strategy upon the colonized peoples." *Science & Society, 37*(2), 129–151.

Mounk, Y. 2022. *The Great Experiment: Why Diverse Democracies Fall Apart and How They Can Endure.* New York: Penguin.

Mudde, C. 2004. "The populist zeitgeist." *Government and Opposition, 39*(4), 541–563.

Mummendey, A., Klink, A. and Brown, R. 2001. "Nationalism and patriotism: National identification and out-group rejection." *British Journal of Social Psychology, 40*(2), 59–172.

Munck, G. L., and Verkuilen, J. 2002. "Conceptualizing and measuring democracy: Evaluating alternative indices." *Comparative Political Studies, 35*(1), 5–34.

Mylonas, H. 2012. *The Politics of Nation-Building: Making Co-nationals, Refugees, and Minorities.* New York: Cambridge University Press.

Mylonas, H. 2015. "Methodological problems in the study of nation-building: Behaviorism and historicist solutions in political science." *Social Science Quarterly, 96*(3), 740–758.

Mylonas, H. 2017. "Nation-building." *Oxford Bibliographies in International Relations.* Ed. Patrick James. New York: Oxford University Press.

Mylonas, H. 2021. "State of Nationalism (SoN): Nation-building." *Studies on National Movements, 8*, 1–17.

Mylonas, H., and Shelef, N. G. 2014. "Which land is our land? Domestic politics and change in the territorial claims of stateless nationalist movements." *Security Studies, 23*(4), 754–786.

Mylonas, H., and Shelef, N. 2017. "Methodological challenges in the study of stateless nationalist territorial claims." *Territory, Politics, Governance, 5*(2), 145–157.

Mylonas, H., and Kuo, K. 2018. "Nationalism and foreign policy." In G. Thies Cameron (ed.), *Oxford Encyclopedia of Foreign Policy Analysis*, New York: Oxford University Press, pp. 223–242.

Mylonas, H., and Whalley, N. 2022. "Pandemic nationalism." *Nationalities Papers*, *50*(1), 3–12.

Mylonas, H., and Radnitz, S. (eds.). 2022. *Enemies within: The Global Politics of Fifth Columns*. New York: Oxford University Press.

Mylonas, H., and Tudor, M. 2021. "Nationalism: What we know and what we still need to know." *Annual Review of Political Science, 24*, 109–132.

Myrdal, G. Sterner, R., Arnold, R. 1944. *An American Dilemma.* (2 vols.). New York: Harper & Bros.

Nairn, T. 2011. *The Enchanted Glass: Britain and Its Monarchy.* London: Verso Books.

Nathanson, S. 1993. *Patriotism, Morality, and Peace.* Lanham, MD: Rowman & Littlefield.

Nielsen, K. 1996. "Cultural nationalism, neither ethnic nor civic." *Philosophical Forum, 28*(1–2).

Nodia, G. 1992. "Nationalism and democracy." *Journal of Democracy, 3*(4), 3–22.

Nozick, R. 1974. *Anarchy, State, and Utopia.* New York, NY: Basic Books.

Onuch, O., and Hale, H. E. 2022. *The Zelensky Effect.* New York: Oxford University Press.

Posen, B. 1993. "Nationalism, the mass army and military power." *International Security, 18*(2), 80–124.

Posner, D. 2005. *Institutions and Ethnic Politics in Africa.* New York: Cambridge University Press.

Posner, D. N. 2017. "When and why do some social cleavages become politically salient rather than others?" *Ethnic and Racial Studies, 40*(12), 2001–2019.

Putin, V. 2021. On the historical unity of Russians and Ukrainians. July 12. http://en.kremlin.ru/events/president/news/66181.

Rafanelli, L. M. 2020. "Toward an individualist postcolonial cosmopolitanism." *Millennium, 48*(3), 360–371.

Rafanelli, L. M. 2021. *Promoting Justice across Borders: The Ethics of Reform Intervention.* New York: Oxford University Press.

Ramet, S. P. 1992. *Balkan Babel: Politics, Culture, and Religion in Yugoslavia.* Boulder, CO: Westview Press.

Renan, E. 1882. *Qu'est-ce qu'une nation?* In Dahbour, O. and Ishay, M. R. (eds). 1995. *The Nationalism Reader.* Atlantic Highlands, NJ: Humanities Press, pp. 143–155.

Rawls, J. 1999. *A Theory of Justice: Revised Edition.* Cambridge, MA: Harvard University Press.

Rawls, J. 1993. "The law of peoples." *Critical Inquiry, 20*(1), 36–68.

Reeskens, T., and Wright, M. 2012. "Nationalism and the cohesive society: A multilevel analysis of the interplay among diversity, national identity, and social capital across 27 European societies." *Comparative Political Studies, 46* (2), 153–181.

Reeskens, T., and Wright, M. 2010. "Beyond the civic-ethnic dichotomy: Investigating the structure of citizenship concepts across thirty-three countries." *Nations and Nationalism, 16*(4), 579–597.

Rhodes, B. 2019. *The World as It is: A Memoir of the Obama White House.* New York: Random House Trade Paperbacks.

Richerson, P., Baldini, R., Bell, A., et al. 2016. "Cultural group selection plays an essential role in explaining human cooperation: A sketch of the evidence." *Behavioral and Brain Sciences*, 39, E30.

Risse, T. 2004. *Social Constructivism and European Integration.* Oxford : Oxford University Press.

Robinson, A. 2014. "National versus ethnic identification: Modernization, colonial legacy, and the origins of territorial nationalism." *World Politics, 66*(4), 709–746.

Rodrik, D. 2006. "Goodbye Washington consensus, hello Washington confusion? A review of the World Bank's economic growth in the 1990s: Learning from a decade of reform." *Journal of Economic Literature, 44*(4), 973–987.

Rokkan, S. 1971. "Nation-building: A review of models and approaches." *Current Sociology, 19*(3), 7–38. https://doi.org/10.1177/001139217101900302.

Romano, D. 2006. *The Kurdish Nationalist Movement: Opportunity, Mobilization and Identity.* New York: Cambridge University Press.

Rosenblatt, P. C. 1964. "Origins and effects of group ethnocentrism and nationalism." *The Journal of Conflict Resolution, 8*(2), 131–146.

Ross, L., and Nisbett, R. E. 2011. *The Person and the Situation: Perspectives of Social Psychology.* London: Pinter & Martin Publishers.

Rotberg, R. I. 1962. "The rise of African nationalism: The case of East and Central Africa." *World Politics, 15*(1), 75–90.

Rutland, A., and Cinnirella, M. 2010. "Context effects on Scottish national and European self-categorization: The importance of category accessibility, fragility and relations." *British Journal of Social Psychology 39*, no. 4: 495–519.

Safran, W. 1990. "The French and their national identity: The quest for an elusive substance?" *French Politics and Society, 8*(1), 56–67.

Sambanis, N., Skaperdas, S., and Wohlforth, W. 2015. "Nation-building through war." *American Political Science Review, 109*(2), 279–296.

Sandel, M. 1998. *Liberalism and the Limits of Justice.* New York: Cambridge University Press.

Sartori, G. 1970. "Concept misformation in comparative politics." *American Political Science Review*, *64*(4), 1033–1053.

Scheffler, S. 2001. *Boundaries and Allegiances: Problems of Justice and Responsibility in Liberal Thought*. New York, NY: Oxford University Press.

Schildkraut, D. 2011. *Americanism in the Twenty-First Century: Public Opinion in the Age of Immigration*. New York: Cambridge University Press.

Sekulić, D., Garth M., and Randy H. 1994. "Who were the Yugoslavs? Failed sources of a common identity in the former Yugoslavia." *American Sociological Review*, *59*(1), 83–97. https://doi.org/10.2307/2096134.

Sekulić, D. 2004. "Civic and ethnic identity: The case of Croatia." *Ethnic and Racial Studies*, *27*, 455–483.

Sewell, W. 1996. "Historical events as transformations of structures: Inventing revolution at the Bastille." *Theory and Society*, 25(6), 841–881.

Shevel, O. 2010. "The post-communist diaspora laws: Beyond the 'good civic versus bad ethnic' nationalism dichotomy." *East European Politics and Societies*, *24*(1), 159–187.

Shevel, O. 2011. *Migration, Refugee Policy, and State Building in Postcommunist Europe*. New York: Cambridge University Press.

Shils, E. 1957. "Primordial, personal, sacred and civil ties: Some particular observations on the relationships of sociological research and theory." *British Journal of Sociology*, *8*(2), 130–145.

Shulman, S. 2002. "Challenging the civic/ethnic and west/east dichotomies in the study of nationalism." *Comparative Political Studies*. *35*(5), 554–585.

Shoup, P. 1962. "Communism, nationalism and the growth of the communist community of nations after World War II." *The American Political Science Review*, *56*(4), 886–898.

Siegelberg, M. 2020. *Statelessness: A Modern History*. Cambridge, MA: University Press.

Simonsen, K. B. and Bonikowski, B. 2020. "Is civic nationalism necessarily inclusive? Conceptions of nationhood and anti-Muslim attitudes in Europe." *European Journal of Political Research*, *59*(1), 114–136.

Singh, P. 2015. *How Solidarity Works for Welfare: Subnationalism and Social Development in India*. New York: Cambridge University Press.

Singer, P. 2004. *One World: Ethics Of Globalisation*. New Delhi: Orient Blackswan.

Sisson, R. and Rose, L. E. 1990. *War and Secession: Pakistan, India, and the Creation of Bangladesh*. University of California Press.

Skey, M., and Antonsich, M. (eds.). 2017. *Everyday Nationhood: Theorising Culture, Identity and Belonging after Banal Nationalism*. Basingstoke: Palgrave Macmillan.

Smith, A. D. 1986. *The Ethnic Origins of Nations.* Oxford: Blackwell.

Smith, A. D. 1991. *National Identity.* Reno, NV: University of Nevada Press.

Smith, A. D. 1995. "Gastronomy or geology? The role of nationalism in the reconstruction of nations." *Nations and Nationalism, 1*(1), 3–23.

Smith, A. D. 1998. *Nationalism and Modernism.* New York: Routledge.

Smith, A. D. 1999. *Myths and Memories of the Nation.* Oxford: Oxford University Press.

Smith, R. 1997. *Civic Ideals: Conflicting Visions of Citizenship in U.S. History.* New Haven, CT: Yale University Press.

Smith, R. 2003. *Stories of Peoplehood: The Politics and Morals of Political Memberships.* New York: Cambridge University Press.

Smith, R. 2015. *Political Peoplehood: The Roles of Values, Interests, and Identities.* Chicago, IL: University of Chicago Press.

Smith, S. C. 2006. "'Moving a little with the tide': Malay monarchy and the development of modern malay nationalism." *The Journal of Imperial and Commonwealth History, 34*(1), 123–138.

Snyder, J. 2000. *From Voting to Violence.* New York: W. W. Norton.

Snyder, L. L. 1976. *Varieties of Nationalism: A Comparative Study.* Holt, Rinehart and Winston.

Somer, M. 2001. "Cascades of ethnic polarization: Lessons from Yugoslavia." *The Annals of the American Academy of Political and Social Science, 573*(1), 127–151.

South, A., and Lall, M. C. 2018. *Citizenship in Myanmar: Ways of Being in and from Burma.* Singapore (Cambridge core).

Spruyt, H. 1994. *The Sovereign State and Its Competitors: An Analysis of Systems Change.* Princeton, NJ: Princeton University Press.

Stepan, A., Linz, J., and Yadav, Y. 2011. *Crafting State-Nations: India and Other Multinational Democracies.* Baltimore, MD: Johns Hopkins University Press.

Stilz, Anna. 2009. *Liberal Loyalty: Freedom, Obligation, and the State.* Princeton, NJ: Princeton University Press.

Stilz, Anna. 2015. "Language, Dignity, and Territory". *Critical Review of International Social and Political Philosophy* 18 (2): 178–190.

Stilz, Anna. 2016. "The Value of Self-Determination." *Oxford Studies in Political Philosophy, 2,* 98–127.

Straus, S. 2015. Making and unmaking nations: War, leadership, and genocide in modern Africa. Ithaca, NY: Cornell University Press.

Suny, R. 1993. *The Revenge of the Past: Nationalism, Revolution, and the Collapse of the Soviet Union.* Stanford: Stanford University Press.

Tajfel, H., and Turner, J. C. 1979. "An integrative theory of intergroup conflict." In W. G. Austin, and S. Worchel (eds.), *The Social Psychology of Intergroup Relations*. Monterey, CA: Brooks/Cole, pp. 33–47.

Tamir, Y. 2020. *Why Nationalism*. Princeton, NJ: Princeton University Press.

Tamir, Y. 2019a. "Not so civic: Is there a difference between ethnic and civic nationalism?" *Annual Review of Political Science*, *22*(1), 419–434.

Tamir, Y. 2019b. "Building a better nationalism: The nation's place in a globalized world." *Foreign Affairs*, *98*(2), 48–53.

Tamir, Y. 1993. *Liberal Nationalism*. Princeton, NJ: Princeton University Press.

Taylor, C. 1992. *The Ethics of Authenticity*. Cambridge, MA: Harvard University Press.

Tilly, C. 1990. *Coercion, Capital and European States, AD 990–1992*. Oxford: Blackwells.

Tilly, C. (ed.). 1975. *The Formation of National States in Western Europe*. Princeton, NJ: Princeton University Press.

Tilly, C., and Blockmans, W. P. (eds.). 1994. *Cities and the Rise of States in Europe, AD 1000 to 1800*. Boulder, CO: Westview Press.

Tishkov, V. A. 2000. "Forget the nation: post-nationalist understanding of nationalism." *Ethnic and Racial Studies*, *23*(4), 625–650.

Theiss-Morse, E. 2009. *Who Counts as an American? The Boundaries of National Identity*. New York: Cambridge University Press.

Tocqueville, A. D. 1835. *Democracy in America*, ed. H. Reeve, F. Bowen, and P. Bradley (tr. H. Reeve 1945). New York: Vintage.

Tudor, M. 2013. *The Promise of Power: The Origins of Democracy in India and Autocracy in Pakistan*. New York: Cambridge University Press.

Tudor, M. 2018. "India's nationalism in historical perspective." *Indian Politics and Policy*, *1*(1), 108–132.

Tudor, M., and Slater, D. 2021. "Nationalism, authoritarianism, and democracy: Historical lessons from South and Southeast Asia." *Perspectives on Politics*, *19*(3), 706–722. https://doi.org/10.1017/S153759272000078X.

Tudor, M. 2023. "Redefined Indian-ness & the decline of India's democracy." In L. Diamond, S. Ganguly, D. Mistree (eds.), *The Troubled State of India's Democracy*, University of Michigan Press.

Valentini, L. 2014. "No global demos, no global democracy? A systematization and critique." *Perspectives on Politics*, *12*(4), 789–807.

Valentini, L. 2013. "Cosmopolitan justice and rightful enforceability." In G. Brock (ed.), *Cosmopolitanism versus Non-Cosmopolitanism: Critiques, Defenses, Reconceptualizations*, Oxford: Oxford University Press, pp. 92–100.

Valdez, I. 2019. *Transnational Cosmopolitanism: Kant, Du Bois, and Justice as a Political Craft*. New York: Cambridge University Press.

Valls, A. 2010. "A liberal defense of black nationalism." *American Political Science Review*, *104*(3), 467–481.

Varshney, A. 1993. "Contested meanings: India's national identity, Hindu nationalism, and the politics of anxiety." *Daedalus*, *122*(3), 227–261.

Viroli, M. 1995. *For Love of Country: An Essay on Patriotism and Nationalism*. London: Clarendon Press.

vom Hau, M. 2009. "Unpacking the school: Textbooks, teachers, and the construction of nationhood in Mexico, Argentina, and Peru." *Latin American Research Review*, *44*(3), 127–154.

Wachtel, A. 1998. *Making a Nation, Breaking a Nation: Literature and Cultural Politics in Yugoslavia*. Stanford, CA: Stanford University Press.

Walzer, M. 1977. *Just and Unjust Wars*. New York: Basic Books.

Walzer, M. 1983. *Spheres of Justice: A Defense of Pluralism and Equality*. New York: Basic Books.

Walzer, M. 2011. "Achieving global and local justice." *Dissent*, *58*(3), 42–48.

Wang, G. (ed.). 2005. *Nation-Building: Five Southeast Asian Histories*. Institute of Southeast Asian Studies.

Weber, E. 1976. *Peasants into Frenchmen: The Modernization of Rural France, 1870–1914*. Stanford, CA: Stanford University Press.

Wedeen, L. 2008. *Peripheral Visions: Publics, Power, and Performance in Yemen*. Chicago, IL: Chicago University Press.

Whitehead, A. L., and Perry, S. L. 2020. *Taking America Back for God: Christian Nationalism in the United States*. New York: Oxford University Press.

Wilkerson, I. 2020. *Caste: The Origins of our Discontents*. New York: Random House.

Williamson, O. E. 2000. "The new institutional economics: Taking stock, looking ahead." *Journal of Economic Literature*, *38*(3), 595–613.

Wimmer, A. 2019. "Why nationalism works: And why it isn't going away." *Foreign Affairs*, *98*, 27–34.

Wimmer, A. 2018. *Nation Building*. Princeton, NJ: Princeton University Press.

Wimmer, A. 2012. *Waves of War: Nationalism, State Formation, and Ethnic Exclusion in the Modern World*. New York: Cambridge University Press.

Wimmer, A., and Feinstein, Y. 2010. "The rise of the nation-state across the world, 1816–2001." *American Sociological Review*, *75*(5), 764–790.

Winichakul, T., 2008. "Nationalism and the radical intelligentsia in Thailand." *Third World Quarterly*, *29*(3), 575–591.

Wittgenstein, L. 2001(1953). *Philosophical Investigations*, trans. G. E. M. Anscombe. Maiden-Berlin: Blackwell.

Woodly, Deva R. 2021. *Reckoning: Black Lives Matter and the Democratic Necessity of Social Movements*. New York: Oxford University Press.

World Bank. 1993. *The East Asian Miracle: Economic Growth and Public Policy*. A World Bank Policy Research Report. London: Oxford University Press

Wright, M., and Citrin, J. 2011. "Saved by the stars and stripes? Images of protest, salience of threat, and immigration attitudes." *American Politics Research*, *39*(2), 323–343.

Wright, M., Citrin, J., and Wand, J. 2012. "Alternative measures of American national identity: Implications for the civic-ethnic distinction." *Political Psychology*, *33*(4), 469–482.

Xenos, N. 1996. "Civic nationalism: oxymoron?" *Critical Review*, *10*(2), 213–231.

Young, C. 1976. *The Politics of Cultural Pluralism*. Madison, Wisconsin: University of Wisconsin Press.

Zaslove, A. 2008. "Exclusion, community, and a populist political economy: The radical right as an anti-globalization movement." *Comparative European Politics*, *6*(2), 169–189.

Zhuravlev, O., and Ishchenko, V. 2020. "Exclusiveness of civic nationalism: Euromaidan eventful nationalism in Ukraine." *Post-Soviet Affairs*, *36*(3), 226–245.

Ziegfeld, A. 2020. "A new dominant party in India? Putting the 2019 BJP victory into comparative and historical perspective." *India Review*, *19*(2), 136–152.

Zimmer, O. 2003. "Boundary mechanisms and symbolic resources: towards a process-oriented approach to national identity." *Nations and Nationalism, 9* (2), 173–193.

Zubrzycki, G. (ed.). 2017. *National Matters: Materiality, Culture, and Nationalism*. Stanford: Stanford University Press.

Zubrzycki, G. 2016. *Beheading the Saint: Nationalism, Religion, and Secularism in Quebec*. Chicago, IL: University of Chicago Press.

Zubrzycki, G. 2001. "'We, the Polish nation': Ethnic and civic visions of nationhood in post-Communist constitutional debates." *Theory and Society*, *30*(5), 629–668.

Acknowledgments

We would like to thank the editors of the Element series, Rachel Beatty Riedl and Ben Ross Schneider, as well as Sultan Alamer, Sophie Blitsman, Nathan Brown, Zeynep Bulutgil, Melani Cammett, Joseph Cerrone, Meghan Garrity, Charlie Glazer, Sam Goldman, Henry Hale, Zaid Hintzman, Eun A Jo, Skyler Kelley-duval, Rachel Kleinfeld, Atul Kohli, Alexander Kolonchin, Debbie Kwak, Ned Lazarus, Karolina Lendák-Kabók, Adam Lenton, Siniša Malešević, Shannon Mallard, Shayon Moradi, Claudia Narberhaus Piera, Takis Pappas, Lucia Rafanelli, Felinda Sharmal, Caleb Schmotter, Sverrir Steinsson, Yuli Tamir, Elpida Vogli, Andreas Wimmer and anonymous reviewers for their helpful comments.

Cambridge Elements ≡

Politics of Development

Rachel Beatty Riedl

Einaudi Center for International Studies and Cornell University
Rachel Beatty Riedl is the Director and John S. Knight Professor of the Einaudi Center for International Studies and Professor in the Government Department and School of Public Policy at Cornell University. Riedl is the author of the award-winning *Authoritarian Origins of Democratic Party Systems in Africa* (2014) and co-author of *From Pews to Politics: Religious Sermons and Political Participation in Africa* (with Gwyneth McClendon, 2019). She studies democracy and institutions, governance, authoritarian regime legacies, and religion and politics in Africa. She serves on the Editorial Committee of World Politics and the Editorial Board of African Affairs, Comparative Political Studies, Journal of Democracy, and Africa Spectrum. She is co-host of the podcast Ufahamu Africa.

Ben Ross Schneider

Massachusetts Institute of Technology
Ben Ross Schneider is Ford International Professor of Political Science at MIT and Director of the MIT-Brazil program. Prior to moving to MIT in 2008, he taught at Princeton University and Northwestern University. His books include *Business Politics and the State in 20th Century Latin America* (2004), *Hierarchical Capitalism in Latin America* (2013), *Designing Industrial Policy in Latin America: Business-Government Relations and the New Developmentalism* (2015), and *New Order and Progress: Democracy and Development in Brazil* (2016). He has also written on topics such as economic reform, democratization, education, labor markets, inequality, and business groups.

Advisory Board

Yuen Yuen Ang, *University of Michigan*
Catherine Boone, *London School of Economics*
Melani Cammett, *Harvard University* (former editor)
Stephan Haggard, *University of California, San Diego*
Prerna Singh, *Brown University*
Dan Slater, *University of Michigan*

About the Series

The Element series *Politics of Development* provides important contributions on both established and new topics on the politics and political economy of developing countries. A particular priority is to give increased visibility to a dynamic and growing body of social science research that examines the political and social determinants of economic development, as well as the effects of different development models on political and social outcomes.

Cambridge Elements ≡

Politics of Development

Elements in the Series

Developmental States
Stephan Haggard

Coercive Distribution
Michael Albertus, Sofia Fenner and Dan Slater

Participation in Social Policy: Public Health in Comparative Perspective
Tulia G. Falleti and Santiago L. Cunial

Undocumented Nationals
Wendy Hunter

Democracy and Population Health
James W. McGuire

Rethinking the Resource Curse
Benjamin Smith and David Waldner

Greed and Guns: Imperial Origins of the Developing World
Atul Kohli

Everyday Choices: The Role of Competing Authorities and Social Institutions in Politics and Development
Ellen M. Lust

Locked Out of Development: Insiders and Outsiders in Arab Capitalism
Steffen Hertog

Power and Conviction:The Political Economy of Missionary Work in Colonial-Era Africa
Frank-Borge Wietzke

Varieties of Nationalism: Communities, Narratives, Identities
Harris Mylonas and Maya Tudor

A full series listing is available at: www.cambridge.org/EPOD

Printed in the United States
by Baker & Taylor Publisher Services